W9-ATG-023

PELÉ

PELÉ

François Thébaud

Translated from the French by Leo Weinstein

HARPER & ROW, PUBLISHERS
New York, Hagerstown, San Francisco, London

This work was originally published in France under the title *Pelé*, © Hatier Paris, 1974.

FIRST EDITION

Designed by C. Linda Dingler

Library of Congress Cataloging in Publication Data

Thébaud, François.
  Pelé.

  1. Nascimento, Edson Arantes do, 1940–
2. Soccer.
GV942.7.N3T4713   796.33′4′0924 [B]   75-30348
ISBN 0-06-014254-5

76 77 78 79 10 9 8 7 6 5 4 3 2 1

CONTENTS

Contents

A section of photographs follows page 56

PREFACE

In the traditional arts, a masterpiece has to await the sovereign verdict of future years or centuries. In soccer, it enjoys the privilege of being immediately recognized as such, because the crowd which consecrates it has, in an unconscious but powerful way, participated in its creation. On the other hand, the only imprint it leaves behind is the image engraven in the memory of those who witnessed it and the signature of its main author.

During the past fifteen years Pelé, the greatest artist in the history of soccer, has signed hundreds of masterpieces, often before movie and television cameras. But what the film has caught is only an imperfect view of living reality, because the wide range of movement of the players on the field is not well suited to the reduced dimensions of the movie screen, let alone the television screen.

No mere writer, even if he has been an enthusiastic witness of Pelé's fabulous career, could pretend to reproduce masterpieces which were, in each case, unpredictable, instantaneous, dazzling syntheses of collective thought and action inspired by this soccer-playing genius.

To recall, through Pelé's history, some of those unforgettable moments when soccer attained the level of art—those seconds that, through the imperfect medium of television, revealed to hundreds of millions of men, women, and children of all countries the magic power of the round ball—this is the task of the first two parts of my book. It is one that has revived nostalgic memories after watching ths first World Cup since 1958 without Pelé.

But the aim of the third, and most important part of this book, is to try to analyze a unique phenomenon: the renown and universal popularity enjoyed by a Black apparently destined for a miserable existence.

For seventeen years I have had the good fortune to watch Pelé perform in the stadiums of Europe and Latin America, and it has been my professional duty to report on him. I have seen him in hotel lobbies and rooms in cosmopolitan centers where his constant globe-trotting led him, as well as in streets and public places. And at Santos too, where his march to glory began in 1956 and where he thought he would put an end to it. Where his family, his friends, his house, his business enterprises are—the backstage setting in which the statements of the player give way to the intimate talk of the man and of those close to him.

Were I to use items of information obtained in this way in order to present an edifying but stupefying image of the "idol," it would be just as dishonest as it would to foster the legend that sometimes depicted him in Europe as a tool of propaganda in the hands of a military dictatorship.

The lover of soccer certainly owes much gratitude to the artist who has offered him so many marvelous emotions. But the best way to show his appreciation is in a clear and objective analysis of the extraordinary social and sports phenomenon Pelé personifies.

F.T.

PART ONE

The Conquest of the World

"Fica! . . . Fica! . . ."—Stay! . . . Stay! . . .

Rising above the deafening noise of the airplanes and helicopters flying above Maracana Stadium, a shout bursts forth from the concrete bowl into which 180,000 spectators are crammed. It is a prayer, a supplication addressed to the dark-skinned athlete who is running an honor lap around the sun-drenched field along the grandstands.

Now, without stopping, the man pulls off his gold-colored shirt, waves it as if he were offering it to the crowd, then brings it down to his face to wipe his eyes, for he is weeping.

On July 18, 1971, Pelé bid adieu to Brazil's national team whose colors, adorned by the now legendary number 10, he has just worn for the 108th time, and to the fans of Rio de Janeiro who had cherished this adopted child of the proud Paulistas far more fiercely than any native Carioca.

One week earlier at Mexico's Azteca Stadium, in a feat never achieved by any other soccer player, Pelé reached the summit of his athletic career—conquering his third World Cup trophy before 105,000 spectators and nearly a billion television viewers. To have participated in a fifth World Cup in 1974—at the age of thirty-

three—would have amounted to running the risk of deceiving 100 million Brazilians for whom the conquest of world supremacy in "futebol" was more important than the assumption of power by a Chief of State.

The prayer of the crowd at Maracana Stadium moved him profoundly, but he did not give way to it. Nor did he change his mind when, at Santos, in February 1974, he received a petition signed by 100,000 schoolchildren and a letter from the Brazilian Federation of Sports urging him to reconsider his decision. He continued to adhere to his position upon learning that the Brazilian government, which does not take matters involving national prestige lightly, urgently wanted him to play for the team coached by Zagalo during the 1974 World Cup in West Germany.

Now that the fourteen-year lease linking his destiny with that of the Brazilian national team had apparently been ended for good, he still had to break his ties with the Santos Futebol Club, whose prestige and receipts depended almost entirely on his presence.

As he told close friends, he wanted that separation to be simple: no planes, no helicopters, no supplications from the crowd, no tears:

"One day soon, during a game, I'll decide that this will be my last one. I'll play until the final whistle. In the dressing room, after the shower, I'll shake hands with my pals, as usual. And I'll say to them: 'Meet Edson Arantes do Nascimento.'"

But although he carried out the first part of this plan in October 1974, he was unable to keep his second promise. For the whole world he remained Pelé. And in June 1975 he accepted a fabulous offer from the American New York Cosmos (7 million for three seasons) and began a new career in New York's Downing Stadium.

1

Edson Arantes do Nascimento

At Tres Coracaoes—The Three Hearts—a small town in the state of Minas Gerais in the interior of Brazil, people were almost unaware of the war that was laying Europe to waste in autumn 1940. For most of its population the horrors of aerial bombings were meaningless reports. Disaster and suffering bore for them the familiar traits of poverty, unemployment, and undernourishment. This mining region, as large as France, contains enormous potential richness and its soil is less arid than that of the Northeast where children are reduced to eating clay, but neither one offers much hope to those unfortunate enough to have been born poor.

Such was the case of Joao Ramos do Nascimento, a Black man with a delicate, open face and solid muscles who, at the age of thirty, had never received any salary other than the 90 cruzeiros he collected at the end of each match played for his local soccer team. Nicknamed Dondinho, he enjoyed a popularity that flattered his carefree personality, but his wife Celeste showed a strong dislike for the profession that provided so badly for her man.

On October 23 that year, when she gave birth to a son, Dondinho was away playing with his team. A week later he made the acquaintance of his offspring and exclaimed delightedly: "With those pretty little thighs he can only become a soccer player!"

His wife replied sourly: "Our little boy is going to be somebody in life, not a vagabond," but Dondinho concluded reflectively: "One can be somebody in life *and* play soccer."

Three years later he would give this child—named Edson and affectionately known as Dico—a rather somber impression of the destiny he had chosen for him.

During a match at Lorena—a town near Lourenço to which the family had then moved, Dondinho was violently tackled by an opponent and sustained a serious knee injury. He was carried home on a stretcher, moaning, in a pitiful state, his wife in tears. His club was too poor to secure more than meager aid in food and money, and there was no question of calling a doctor.

Now the family, with the addition of a second boy, suffered the horrors of extreme poverty. After weeks of inactivity Dondinho was reduced to menial tasks to assure the survival of his loved ones.

When he finally recovered, he jumped avidly at the chance offered him by a club in the state of Bauru, near Sao Paulo, of a position on its team and an additional small job in the municipal service.

For the first time Celeste Arantès would see her life's dream come true: her husband provided with a "serious," stable profession that guaranteed their daily dish of "feijaoes" (black beans).

The entire family set out for the promised land and set up quarters in a small, one-story house with ocher-colored tiles and a chalk-white front in a workers' quarter of Bauru.

It was here in "September 7" Street that Edson discovered "futebol" along with the neighborhood kids. And a long time before going to school, since this was a privilege reserved for families capable of paying for an education which, in Brazil, is neither compulsory nor free.

On the "field" marked out by the sidewalks, cans serving as goalposts, the game played by the street urchins of Bauru bore at best only a vague resemblance to the sport codified by soccer's International Board. The ball was a round bundle of rags held together by strings, since a rubber ball was a luxury as inaccessible to the kids as shoes.

Still, from dusk to dawn, the street was the arena for noisy, hard-fought games in which Edson participated passionately. And when, giving in to his mother, who had other ambitions for him, Edson became a pupil, he resolved the classical conflict between duty and passion with far less hesitation than Corneille's heroes—choosing soccer.

Bitter reproaches, moral coercion, slaps, threats, all drew from him only a few temporary concessions. For this boy already displayed a strong personality, encouraged, admittedly, by his father's sympathy. In the street he was called "Dondinho's son," which presumably did not leave his soccer-playing father indifferent.

Was he the one who conceived the original idea of organizing a sale of roasted peanuts to raise money for a real ball? At any rate, he participated actively in a bold scheme which consisted of carrying off part of a shipment of peanuts piled up in a freight car in the station, and then toasting them in the crumbling cave of an abandoned house. The enterprise was carried out successfully. Now the team of September 7 had a ball and a set of old, faded uniforms. This represented a fortune until the day one of the cave walls gave way, burying a child beneath the rubble.

Edson said later: "When my buddy's mother saw her son's dead body, she was in the kitchen with her hands in flour. I think I'll never forget the terrible sight of her black face with the tears and streaks of flour running down. I couldn't stand it and ran away like a thief."

Aside from this drama, the conflicts between Edson and his friends and the property owners of September 7 Street were the usual ones: broken windows, the area plunged into darkness after an unforeseen encounter between the ball and a high-tension wire, chases and pulled ears—every child in the world has gone through such tragicomedies.

But the sequel to the adventures of Edson and his gang was more characteristic of poor children's lives in Brazil.

One day they received a visit from an "impresario" who proposed, just like that, to turn the gang into a professional team, saying he would take care of the equipment and the salaries.

Tempted by the "remuneration" of 4.50 cruzeiros, they accepted and began to transform the social status of the club. Henceforth it would bear the name "Ameriquinha" Little America, which sounded more serious.

They were a little taken back on realizing that the shoes with cleats promised by the "impresario" were old, used "chuteiras" bought at a ridiculous price from the real adult professionals of Bauru A.C., the local club. But since wearing new shoes would have caused problems for kids who had never worn shoes anyway, they were ready to overlook this detail. Besides, the idea of playing on a real field against real teams was enough to make them forget all the rest.

The small-time impresario had flair. His boys easily won the "infanto juvenil" championship of Bauru, watched by interested idlers who hung around the vacant lots where the games were played. Dondinho, admiring his son's exploits, was so happy after the final victory that he walked him home and gave him a warm hug. Edson received a bonus of 36 cruzeiros and went on his first spree that night to squander this fortune with his teammates on heaps of ice cream and Coca-Cola.

For two years he brought success to the "Ameriquinha" Club and its impresario. With his frail thighs, the skinny adolescent looked unimpressive, but his skill in shooting, his ease in feinting and dribbling, his quick starts, and his stamina could not escape the eyes of a connoisseur, and there happened to be one in Bauru —Valdemar de Brito. A friend of Dondinho's, de Brito was a former soccer player who had had his hour of glory on Brazil's national team. Now the coach for Bauru A.C., he signed up Edson, gave him advice, and helped him perfect his technique. As a result the "infanto juvenil" team, called the "Bacquinho," carried off three regional championships, thanks chiefly to his favorite pupil who scored 40 goals in fifteen games.

De Brito was sold. This kid nicknamed "Pelé" by his comrades (perhaps because he revealed his qualities in "peladas," pick-up games played on vacant lots) definitely had what it took to go far.

In Dondinho, de Brito then found the indispensable ally to persuade Celeste Arantès, who was still convinced that as a profession "futebol" meant starvation and that little Dico should be steered away from it at any price.

The struggle was uneven. After strenuous resistance, she gloomily accepted the decision that her favorite son should attempt the venture in which his father had failed so dismally.

At Santos, 312 miles from Bauru, Valdemar de Brito had asked the coach of one of the greatest Brazilian clubs to grant a tryout to his young discovery.

The whole family accompanied the conqueror to Bauru station. Our skinny hero of fifteen had little going for him. Lost in his first pair of long pants taken from his father's wardrobe, suffocating from the pressure of his first tie knot, ill at ease in his first pair of dress shoes, the emotion of this separation from his family and fear of the unknown made him burst into tears when his father put his small cardboard suitcase on the baggage rack.

During the trip a drunkard sat down opposite him and, pointing a trembling index finger at him, said:

"I know you, you are Dondinho's son. I read in the newspaper that you were going to try your luck at Santos. Well, well, I was a professional player too and everything went well till the day someone broke my leg. After that, everybody abandoned me. Look out! You may turn out like me!"

Dico's morale was at its lowest when he met Valdemar de Brito at Sao Paulo station. Without so much as a greeting he said: "I don't want to go to Santos. I'm taking the first train back to Bauru."

Nevertheless, he took the "onibus" to Santos. The little boy from the provinces was so fascinated by the spectacle of white skyscrapers, feverish traffic in the streets, and crowds hurrying on the sidewalks that he left a good portion of his anxieties in the winding Via Ancheta which leads down from Sao Paulo to the port and the beaches of Santos.

No sooner had they arrived than de Brito took him to the Vila Beleiro Stadium so that the boy could watch his future team-mates work out. But the virtuosity and above all the size of these "idols" only renewed the fears that had assailed him on the trip.

His "manager's" reassurances had no effect on him—he had made up his mind: "I'll work out with them and then I'll return to Bauru."

Next day, in the stadium dressing room he was introduced to the Santos players, but felt no more confident despite the friend-liness shown him by Zito, Pepe, and Vasconcellos, those demi-gods he had never dreamed of shaking by the hand.

On the playing field, wet from a persistent rain, his 130-pound frame lost in a shirt too large for him and faced with a ball as slippery as a bar of soap, it was a nightmare. Everything he did seemed awkward and ridiculous compared with the feats those giants of soccer accomplish with such ease. Used to playing on dry, dusty grounds, he lost his balance several times on the soaked turf. His passes seemed so inaccurate that he dared not attempt a feint, a dribble, or a shot. It was a fiasco. So convinced was he that, back in the dressing room after the training session, he was stupefied when Lula, the coach, said to him: "You still have a lot to learn. You have to gain some weight before you'll be ready to play in the First Division. But if you want to, we'll prepare your contract today."

Yet the "saudade" remained—that melancholy experienced by every displaced person which he could not shake off. Two or three days later he left for Bauru, on the pretext that he had to get his personal effects and wanted to say goodbye to his par-ents, who had read of their son's promotion in the local press.

Back in familiar surroundings, with his pals, his childhood memories, and his mother—who had never resigned herself to their separation—he decided to stay home.

Three weeks later Valdemar de Brito showed up, shouting and admonishing: "You're not a kid any more but a player on one of Brazil's most famous professional teams, which will soon offer you a monthly salary of 6,000 cruzeiros and the possibility of becoming a 'star.' Could you be stupid enough to throw away a chance like that?"

The lesson struck home. Edson do Nascimento packed his bags and took the train to São Paulo.

Several years later he said: "That day I became a man."

2

The Birth of Pelé

In August 1955 Edson was not quite fifteen. To the stars of Santos Futebol Club he was just a kid, "um garoto," who acted as their errand boy when they wanted a pack of cigarettes or a snack. Since he admired them too much to take offense and did his job with zeal, they ironically called him "Gasolina."

By now Dondinho's son had adapted perfectly to his milieu. He lived in a modest boardinghouse, where the club had placed him along with some other young players, including Dorval, a Black. Between training sessions and matches he took courses to fill the numerous gaps in his scholastic knowledge. And every month he proudly sent almost his entire salary to his mother, for the bonus money he received for the games won with the "juveniles" team and later with the "aspirantes" was enough to cover this serious adolescent's modest needs.

On the playing field he gained in self-confidence, and as a result of growth and training his muscles were developing. Coach Lula paid special attention to the young players, for his professional team contained several veterans who were approaching retirement.

On September 7, 1956—by a strange coincidence the date which marks National Independence Day was also the name of the street of his home in Bauru—Edson made the "big time" during a game played by the Santos club at Santo André. When

Tite, the regular left wing, was injured in the second half, Lula decided to have Pelé replace him.

The stadium announcer knew his "futebol" history. Forced to name a substitute, he came out with that of a well-known Brazilian player who was not a member of Santos: Telé. As for the referee, when Pelé reported, he condescendingly looked over the presumptuous adolescent who claimed the right to participate in this grown-up battle.

However, he forgot his prejudices when the newcomer, moving instantaneously for one of those unpredictable passes that earned Jair his glory, took possession of the ball in the opponent's penalty area, eliminated a defender with a masterful swerve, and beat the goalie of Santo André with a cannon shot. Only later, much later, would this referee learn that he was in charge of a historic game—the one that opened the most formidable series of goals ever scored by a soccer player.

Lula knew his job too well to take into his regular line-up a player not yet ripe for the tough matches of the Paulista League games. But every time circumstances permitted, when his team was securely ahead, he made him enter the game in the second half in place of a tired regular.

Thus a tour through Rio Grande do Sul early in 1957 enabled Pelé to occupy, one by one, the positions held by Del Vecchio, Jair, Pagao, and Tite, who made up the typical forward line of Santos. And nearly every time he inscribed his name among the goal scorers.

He had a total of 8 to his credit when Lula decided the time had come to give him a regular starting position. On April 26, in Pacaembu Stadium in Sao Paulo, Pelé made his official debut against Sao Paulo F.C. in the annual tournament which pits the great clubs of the two neighboring states against each other. Santos won by 3–1 and the Paulista press discovered Pelé. In right-wing position he eliminated three opponents while running with lightning speed along the touchline, veered toward the center, faked a pass to Del Vecchio, and slipped the ball past the goalie from a closed angle as the crowd rose to acclaim this feat.

A month later, against Palmeiras, the other great Paulista rival, Santos came out on top, 3–0. Pelé scored 2 goals. Now the machine had been set in motion. In a friendly game against Lavras, he scored four times!

On May 29 he played for the first time in Maracana, the gigantic stadium in Rio, and received an ovation from more than 100,000 spectators, having played a major part in the crushing victory of Santos over America of Rio (4–0). In that game he again scored a brilliant goal.

Pelé made such an impression on the Cariocas that Vasco da Gama, one of the great clubs of the capital, requested his participation and that of several other Santos players to form a "combinado" of the two clubs in a tournament organized in Maracana Stadium to which Belenenses Lisbon and Dynamo Zagreb had been invited. Pelé scored 3 of the 6 goals against the Portuguese, 1 against the Yugoslavs, 1 against Sao Paulo, and 1 against Flamengo—a total of 6 goals in four games!

There was another side to the coin in the growing reputation of this sixteen-year-old player. The defenders of the teams he played used increasingly rough tactics to stop him, for his speed and variety of feints confronted them with problems they could not solve. During a match against Flamengo, the irascible Carioca fullback Pavao lost his temper and tried to strike him. Jair was expelled for taking up his defense.

In the Paulista championship—the big attraction of the second half of 1957—the provincial teams, weaker than their opponents, frequently resorted to violence to make up for their technical inferiority when facing the big clubs: Sao Paulo F.C., Palmeiras, Corintians, Portuguesa, and, naturally, Santos.

During a game of this sort Pelé, booed by some of the spectators every time he touched the ball, scored a sensational goal near the stands where most of the fanatical fans were seated. He jumped high in front of his critics, raised his arm, and struck the air with his closed fist—a gesture of triumph and defiance that would be repeated later in every stadium in the world.

Now nothing could stop the meteoric rise of this young forward, increasingly sure of himself and obviously endowed with exceptional qualities. Santos finished the championship games in second place behind Palmeiras as 1957 drew to a close. But with a total of 36 goals, Pelé was the top "artilhero" of the competition. His record added up to 65 goals since he first wore the colors of his club.

Silvio Pirilo, who selected the national team, had already been struck by the extraordinary effectiveness of the player Santos had only recently made a regular. But there was great surprise when he decided to pick Pelé for the Brazilian squad that would play Argentina in the Rocca Cup, in two games as the rules provided.

The critics came down hard on Pirilo:

"A sixteen-year-old playing against opponents as tough as Argentina . . . it's madness! Anyway, who is Pelé?"

Pelé's reply was to score the only goal for Brazil—who were defeated 2–1—having replaced his Santos teammate Del Vecchio in the second half. And he played the entire return match which Brazil won (2–0) in Sao Paulo. There he scored his second goal in an international game.

The year 1957 had shown what the young player could do. When Pelé set out on the campaign of 1958, his reputation was already established in the great soccer centers of his country.

In a game against Corintians, the most popular club of Sao Paulo, Pelé scored Santos's 3 goals. To console the losers, someone in the dressing room yelled: "There's never been a soccer player of such class in Brazil!"

Not all Brazilians shared this opinion, even though Pelé drove home one or more "goles" for Santos in each game of the 1958 Paulista championship competition. While his muscles had filled out his body, many still considered him too "tender" to face baptism in the World Cup, to be held in Sweden in June.

He had no difficulty in confounding the critics in the friendly matches against Paraguay and Bulgaria played in preparation for the World Cup. One goal in the net in the first match, 2 past the goalie in the second—surely this seventeen-year-old had what it took to silence the skeptics and arouse the enthusiasm of the crowds at Maracana Stadium.

But when he boarded the plane for Stockholm, Pelé was suffering from a knee injury received from Ari Clemente, a full-back for the Corintians, whom Pelé had faced in a training match a few days before leaving.

His absence was scarcely noticed in the first two games Brazil played in the World Cup. First, because European observers had not heard much of Pelé; and second, because the South American team had created a sensation since arriving in Europe. On its way through Italy, the Brazilians crushed two of the peninsula's most feared teams, Fiorentina and Juventus, by identical scores of 4–0; and they kept up the momentum in their first World Cup game by handing Austria a convincing 3–0 defeat at Uddevalla Stadium.

But against England, in the magnificent Göteborg Stadium, the Brazilian artillery sputtered. Joel Mazzola,[1] Vava, and Zagalo came down a notch and could not manage to beat goal-keeper MacDonald. This disappointing game ended in a scoreless tie (0–0). Vicente Feola, technical director of the selection, decided to replace Joel and Mazzola by Garrincha and Pelé in the match against Wales that would decide who was to qualify for the Quarter-Finals.

Feola's choice proved correct. The fierceness of the Welsh defenders presented the Brazilian forwards with the same problem as the strength of the English defenders. But this time the Brazilians had the solution. During one of the numerous melées in the penalty area brought on by the massive retreat of the Welsh and the Brazilian pressure, Pelé received a high pass from a teammate. He controlled the ball with his chest, let it drop on his foot, lifted it over the opponent attacking him, and, without

1. Mazzola was later transferred to Italy, where he plays under the name of Altafini—Translator's note.

letting it touch the ground, blasted it past petrified goalkeeper Kelsey. It was the only goal of the game. But what a goal! Now Brazil could pursue the road to conquest of the World Cup that had eluded it in 1950 before 200,000 horrified Cariocas.

In the Semi-finals the French team was the opponent—a team whose forward line (Wisnieski-Kopa-Fontaine-Vincent) had been sensationally effective, scoring 15 goals in four games and which had reached the Semi-finals with a solid 4–0 victory over Northern Ireland, who had unexpectedly eliminated Argentina and Czechoslovakia.

But the tricolored defense was not up to the caliber of its attack. From the opening whistle on, it showed signs of nervousness which, in the second minute, led to a bad pass by Jonquet. Garrincha immediately took advantage of the error and his sharp center enabled Vava to open the scoring. The French forwards reacted admirably. Kopa dribbled past three defenders, creating a breach in the Brazilian defense into which Fontaine slipped to beat goalkeeper Gilmar to the ball and fire a cross shot that ended up in the net.

But the equal score could not reassure the French defenders. Jonquet was injured in a collision with Vava while trying to recover a ball lost from overeagerness. Though suffering from a fractured shin, he went on playing but had to retire from the game after 45 minutes. With only ten players, the French could not restrain the inspired Brazilians. A marvelous curved shot, the famous "folha seca" (dry leaf) by Didi, fooled the French goalie Abbes before the intermission. And during the second half Pelé received enthusiastic applause from the Stockholm spectators by tallying 3 goals, each a jewel of technique.

This time the word *Pelé*, riding the radio waves and printed in all the newspapers, made its first trip around the world. Everywhere fans started to pronounce the two-syllabled nickname of a seventeen-year-old Black with delicate muscles and slender frame who seemed almost joyfully to overcome all obstacles.

A star was born!

In the final game between Brazil and Sweden, for some quar-

ter of an hour the Scandinavians roused false hopes in their supporters. The bitter memory of the unhappy 1950 Final still
preyed on those who had succeeded Jair, Ademir, Zizinho, and
the others who lost at Maracana. Thanks to the phlegmatic Liedholm, the Swedes even drew first blood, applauded by 60,000
delighted spectators. But the Brazilians shook off their torpor and
Vava scored 2 goals on identical outflanking maneuvers by Garrincha. Despite its advantage on the scoreboard, the Brazilian
team was not without forebodings. Once again Pelé exorcized its
fears by succeeding with another "chapeau" (hat), the same technical feat that had enabled it to eliminate Wales. Gustavsson, the
solid Swedish center half, and goalie Svensson, mystified in almost the same fraction of a second, saw the ball only when it hit
the back of the net. Freed of their anxieties, the Brazilians concluded the dazzling ballet begun against France. With goals by
Zagalo and again Pelé, they defeated their opponents by the
same score they had inflicted on the French: 5–2.

Bellini, the magnificent blond athlete who anchored the Brazilian defense, received the golden statuette of winged victory—
symbol of world supremacy in soccer—from the hands of the
Swedish king. As he raised it above his head in offering to the
crowd, in a gesture which the gigantic statue erected in front of
the entrance to Maracana Stadium would later recall for poster-
ity, Pelé, Garrincha, and Zagalo wept for joy.

In Rio, where the whole town had been riveted to their radio
sets, people danced wild sambas in every street.

Gooool do Pelé! . . . Gooool do Pelé! . . .

The long, joyous shout of ecstatic radio reporters was taken
up by the crowd.

A seventeen-year-old kid had just made the dream of an entire people come true.

3

The 1,000-Goal Man

In soccer the world champions only defend their title once every four years. But for the player who has contributed to capturing it, every match, even a scrimmage, turns henceforth into a test to prove that he is not just an ordinary performer. All the more so if he hails from a country whose history contains few martial exploits and which suddenly scores a triumph that swells national pride. And still more if the hero of this modern and peaceful epic is a lad of seventeen whose humble origins underline his brilliant feat.

On his return from Sweden Pelé did not stop to reflect whether it is more difficult to hold one's ground than to conquer.

As if it were the most natural thing in the world, he was going to set a record that still stands today: scoring 58 goals in the Sao Paulo championship games. Four times he put in 4 goals in a game, once 5; five times he hit for 3. These are incredible achievements when we consider that they were performed against provincial teams that play "the match of their life" when hosting a great club like Santos, or against a club as prestigious as the Corintians of Sao Paulo.

In 1959, although top scorer of the Paulista League for the third consecutive time, Pelé had notched "only" 46 goals. But his total for the year amounted to 126, two-thirds of them scored in games abroad for the Brazilian national team and Santos.

In March Brazil participated in the South American Championship, the traditional tournament of the continent's national teams. This year the games were held in Buenos Aires in an atmosphere of tension. Uruguay and Argentina, humiliated by elimination from, or bad showing in, the 1958 World Cup, had particular motivation to regain their lost prestige by a victory over the world championship team.

Right from the kickoff of their game against Brazil the Uruguayans, whose aggressive play is legendary, triggered the most frightful pitched battle ever seen on a soccer field. Nearly 200 people, including substitutes, trainers, photographers and, of course, the players, were involved in an enormous scuffle. Pelé, overcome by the situation (he was not yet nineteen), was one of the first victims. Calm was restored only after the police intervened and four players had been sent off the field. Then Brazil won 3–1, but the young star had not played an important role in the victory.

This dramatic match would influence the final standings of the competition. Held to a tie by Peru, due to overconfidence, the Brazilian team, intimidated by the ring of police around the field with guns pointed at the spectators, settled for another tie in the Final against Argentina. Brazil had saved its invincibility but lost the "Sud-Americano."

Nevertheless, the Buenos Aires press voted Pelé the most valuable player of the tournament, in which he had been top scorer with 9 goals in seven games.

Pelé's the best! The verdict was unanimous, not only in South America but in Europe too. Santos F.C., in demand everywhere because it featured the man universally called "the phenomenon of soccer," multiplied its tours. Bulgaria, Belgium, Holland, Germany, Italy, Spain . . . The team in white jerseys covered the old continent and, not content just to exhibit its "phenomenon," produced magnificent soccer while slaughtering its opponents.

Hannover and Inter Milan allowed 7 goals, Hamburg 6, Feyenoord 3, Barcelona 5, Valencia 4. As for Pelé, he scored 28 of the 69 goals netted by Santos on its first swing through Europe.

This extraordinary success meant that the Santos officials placed an ever greater importance on tours which had turned out to be far more lucrative than games played at home. But one clause was contained in every contract: Santos's take would be cut in half if Pelé did not play. And this despite the fact that its line-up included two other members of the world championship team (Gilmar and Zito), as well as newly capped players Mengalvio, Calvet, Lima, Pepe, Dorval, and Mauro.

At this point Pelé's career entered its second phase: the one in which money took on an important role. Until now financial matters had had only limited interest for him. His meteoric rise on the sports scene had brought him a considerable increase in salary and bonus payments. Once he realized that he was the principal source of the annual income of a club that lived on a large scale, once extravagant transfer offers flocked in and the press in every country called Santos the "Pelé Football Club," why shouldn't he demand his share of the pie?

These new preoccupations did not interfere with Pelé's performance. During its 1960 European tour, Santos went goal-crazy: among others, 7 in Malmoe, 10 in Antwerp, 5 in Warsaw (against the Polish national team), 5 and 4 in Paris against Reims and Racing Paris, 9 in Munich. Pelé was everywhere: 5 goals here, 4 there, 3 somewhere else—and everywhere there were enthusiastic crowds. Then, on returning home, 32 goals in the Paulista championship games!

In 1961 the tours continued with the same success. The Pelé F.C. was in demand everywhere. Nevertheless, Santos also managed to win the Sao Paulo League title and then the first all-Brazilian championship. That year Pelé scored 111 goals, a little less than in 1959 but considerably more than in 1960 (75).

No wonder that Pelé's body, subjected to such effort, exerted between continuous long, tiring trips, muscles forced to adapt to abrupt changes of climate and food, would one day crack up.

The drama occurred in June 1962 in Chile, at the Sausalito Stadium in Vina del Mar on the Pacific shore, where Brazil was defending the world title it had won at Stockholm in 1958.

Feola's successor as technical director of the "amarela" (gold and green) selection, Aimoré Moreira, had not dared replace members of the team that won in Sweden. Nine of them had been kept in the line-up.

The opening match of this aging squad was painful. Although Mexico, their opponent, was a mediocre team, the Brazilians experienced difficulties in keeping up the pace they tried to impose. Pelé had to come up with two quick thrusts to wake up the spectators and lead his team to victory.

A few days later a disappointed Chilean crowd witnessed a similiar spectacle during the Brazil–Czechoslovakia match. Clearly, Pelé alone had the capacity to make the "difference." So he set out to do so. After a violent shot that hit the crossbar of the Czech goal, just as he was poised for a second shot, the surprised spectators saw him suddenly stop in full motion, put his hands on his lower abdomen, and collapse to the turf. The trainer rushed out and signaled for help. Pelé was carried off the field, his face contorted with pain. The immediate medical diagnosis: a deep muscle pull. The prognosis (carefully kept from his teammates so as not to hurt their morale): Pelé was out for this World Cup and even for weeks thereafter.

The young Amarildo replaced him and saved Brazil's qualification by defeating a stubborn Spanish team led by Puskas. Garrincha took on the decisive role in the Quarter-final against England and the Semi-final against Chile. In the Final, Czechoslovakia with its slow pace offered the "old" Brazilians ideal conditions in which to show what they had left in them. Didi, Zito, Vava, Nilton Santos, and Mauro even seemed to discover a second youth, and they retained the World Cup. Pelé, who had shared the anguish of his teammates in the stands, embraced Amarildo—whose subsequent career would prove that he surpassed himself in Chile.

At the end of August, three months after the drama of Vina del Mar, Pelé returned to the Santos line-up. He scored another 37 goals in the Paulista League games, participated in a brilliant European tour where he beat the goalies of Hamburg and Racing

Paris seven times in two games, and played a decisive role in the victory of Santos in the South American Champions' Cup. Then on to the Intercontinental Cup (the unofficial world championship of clubs), where he scored 5 goals against Benfica after having caused a sensation in Lisbon by winding his way through the excellent Portuguese defense as if on exercise in a training session.

Was the injury of Vina del Mar no more than a bad memory? The torn muscle that kept him from playing had completely healed, but in a type of soccer that had become more and more physical as a result of the "win at any price" philosophy, the knees, ankles, and shins of such a dangerous forward became the habitual target of "realistic" defenders. Pelé's muscular build had gained in strength. With a weight of 165 lbs. and a height of 5 feet 9 inches, his impressive thighs, large shoulders and powerful chest, this magnificent athlete did not have to fear the toughest tackles. And when circumstances obliged him to face up to an opponent, his lightning starts, his "take-off" for heading, and his quick reflexes were factors that made "dirty players" think twice before taking him on. But his muscular joints were as vulnerable as those of any other soccer player.

When, in 1963, the Brazilian national team went on a European tour, he was hampered by an injury. And even though he came off the bench twice to save the seriously tarnished prestige of the world champions (against France where he scored the 3 goals that won the game, and against Germany where he hit for 1 of the 2 goals of the win), he was not in top condition.

With Santos, too, he played only one of the three games of the Intercontinental Cup Final which his club captured for the second time by defeating Milan. But he contributed to the triumph by scoring 2 goals in Milan's San Siro Stadium in the first-leg game.

Pelé's performance in 1964 would be diminished by three injuries that kept him out of several games. The total number of goals scored was the smallest since he began his career at Santos (60, of which 34 were in the Paulista League matches). Nevertheless, in November he achieved a feat unique in the records of soccer history: he scored 8 goals against Botafogo de Riberao Preto in an official league game. And to prove that this was not a fluke, he followed it up by smashing in 4 goals against Corintians, again in a league match, and 3 against Fluminense.

Accomplished at the end of the year, these feats held the promise of a new start. And indeed, in 1965 Pelé enjoyed one of his best seasons, with 105 goals to his credit, 49 of them in Paulista League matches.

So great was his prestige by now that Rio de Janeiro, Belo Horizonte, and Santos all bestowed on him the title of honorary citizen. Robert Kennedy, after watching him play at Maracana Stadium, came into the dressing room and embraced him with the soapy water still streaming down his face.

Sir Stanley Rous—British president of the International Soccer Federation (FIFA) and thus director of the organization of the 1966 World Cup, which this time took place in England— had reserved a curious reception for the "genius."

Pelé was in remarkable form at the start of the World Cup. He had proved it in the warm-up games of the Brazilian national team (10 goals in six games). But the referees at Liverpool, chosen by Sir Stanley Rous, had definite instructions to go easy on the "virile" game of the European teams. Right at the first appearance of the Brazilian team against Bulgaria, this led to repeated and unpunished aggressions by the Bulgarian defender Jetchev against Pelé. Still, Pelé scored 1 of the 2 goals of the Brazilian victory. But he was not fit to play the second match, which Brazil lost to Hungary. Although not fully recovered, he took his place in the line-up against Portugal in order to try to save the endangered qualification. And he fell under the blows coldly aimed at his knee by "the killer" Morais who, in front of 80,000 indignant and horrified spectators, as well as millions of television viewers, committed one of the most scandalous acts in the history of sport.

While all South America hurled its indignation at the un-sportsmanlike maneuvers that had brought about the elimination of its three representatives (Brazil, Argentina, and Uruguay) and facilitated the final victory of the English national team, Pelé, back at Santos, drew the lesson to be learned from the violence at Liverpool.

Six weeks later, his knee still hurting, he returned to play for the Santos team, which needed him more and more. But the heart had gone out of him and, although he notched 37 goals before the season was over, his smile was gone. The role of eternal globe-trotter began to weigh on him. The advertising contracts which brought him substantial revenues demanded his attention. Santos neglected national competitions in favor of more lucrative foreign tours. The United States, Africa, the Near East, and Asia all paid enormous sums to see the Pelé Football Club in action.

Pelé honored his contracts and his reputation as "hombre-gol" (goal man). Without straining, in each game he performed a few of the tricks that only he could manage. But the drama of Liverpool had left its mark on him. And he told me confidentially in the Santos dressing room: "For me there will be no more World Cups. Soccer has been distorted by violence and destructive tactics. I don't want to end up an invalid."

By 1969 he had recovered his gusto—the 4 goals he put into the net of an opponent as tough as Botafogo were an unmistakable sign of it.

And when the new selector Joao Saldanha revealed his plan to choose Tostao as his partner in the middle of the forward line of the national team for the World Cup elimination games, Pelé agreed to participate in the adventure. The perfect understanding on the field between these two "Mineiros" (Tostao also is a native of the state of Minas Gerais) resulted in six splendid victories. Brazil qualified triumphantly for the final round. Tostao registered 10 of the 28 goals allowed by Colombia, Venezuela, and Paraguay, and Pelé's name appeared five times on the scoreboard.

These two soccer "brains" were born to understand one another. The dark clouds looming over the future of the Brazilian team had been dispersed by the tremendous enthusiasm unleashed at these brilliant results, justly attributed to "Pelé-Tostao."

Already a record entitled "The Man-Eaters on the Road to Mexico" led the hit parade. It contained excerpts from televised play-by-play reports in which the famous sportscaster Valdir Amaral described the goals of the Brazilian team in its qualification games. "Gooool do Tostao! . . . Gooool do Pelé! . . ." Between samba refrains the interminable cry of victory resounds like a song of hope.

Brazil's ambition now was to accomplish the exploit of capturing the World Cup for the third time, and so finally gain possession of the golden statuette with the name of Jules Rimet, founder of the competition, on its base.

4

A King Elected by the World

For Pelé the year 1969 would end on November 19.

Toward the middle of October the Brazilian press, checking its statistics, discovered that the total number of goals he had scored since the beginning of his career was approaching 1,000. When we consider that Jimmy MacGrory of the Glasgow Celtics acquired immortal glory in Great Britain for having registered 500 goals at a time when defenses were far less reinforced, we can get some idea of the significance of this.

Brazilian public opinion took fire. On October 22, at Curitiba, Pelé scored his 995th goal. Henceforth a swarm of telereporters, radiomen, newspaper reporters, and photographers from international agencies took up the hunt for "Goal No. 1,000." Santos, down in the standings of the national league games which the club had neglected completely, held no interest for them. What mattered was to be there when Pelé reached the fateful four-digit number!

On November 1, against Flamengo at Rio, he raised his total to 996. On the 13th, against Santa-Cruz at Recife, 2 goals brought the count to 998. It rose to 999 on the 14th at Paraiba. Would it be pulled off at Bahia, in the Fonte Nova Stadium where he was playing his next match? The whole nation was glued to transistor radios. At the shore of All Saints' Bay that inspired Jorge Amado, everything was ready to celebrate the event with a splendor that would put the Cariocas who had hoped it would happen in Rio to shame. Even a thanksgiving Mass had been included in the program of popular rejoicing.

Apparently Pelé did all he could to satisfy the expectations of the densest Black population in any Brazilian town. A few seconds before the final whistle he cut through the Bahia defense, getting off a shot in full motion that had the goalie beat. The ball hit the crossbar and bounced back onto the playing field. Pelé was about to follow up and put it into the empty goal. His teammate Jair Bala, better placed, got there first and scored the winning goal for Santos.

The Cariocas could thank the humble substitute, since the next match on the Santos schedule was at Maracana Stadium, where they were to meet Vasco da Gama on November 19.

On D-Day torrential rain poured down on Rio.

No matter—80,000 Cariocas preferred to witness the event first-hand rather than staying home where all the TV channels offered them close-ups of the game.

In the gigantic Rio Stadium all eyes were of course fixed on the Santos player who wore the number 10. The movement of the ball was of interest only when it came near him. Pelé was closely guarded by René, the Black defender for Vasco da Gama, who towered over him and tackled so vigorously that he hardly touched a ball.

Visibly nervous, Pelé tried to escape from this surveillance, but René's tentacular legs were always quicker. It took half an hour before Pelé succeeded in a feint that temporarily fooled his opponent and followed it up with a superb lob shot. Andrada, the international Argentine goalie for Vasco, took a desperate leap and managed to push the ball over the crossbar with his fingertips.

A few minutes later another shot by Pelé, full force this time, hits the crossbar. Then with the whole crowd on its feet, just as he prepares to slam home a high center, René's head intervenes to smash the ball into the net for a self-goal. A goal that satisfies Santos but certainly not the crowd, which boos the killjoy.

The nervous tension increases in the arena as the spectators feverishly check the time remaining for play. Finally a defense-splitting pass by Clodoaldo, a lightning take-off by Pelé between René and Fernando . . . The two Vasco defenders are left behind. Unhesitatingly Fernando trips Pelé in the midst of the penalty area.

When, after long concentration, Pelé succeeds in curving in the penalty kick on a low shot preceded by a feint, all hell breaks loose. The field is invaded by hundreds of reporters and photographers, who first keep Pelé imprisoned in Andrada's goal, then carry him on their shoulders in triumph. The crowd demands an honor lap which he does after having put on a jersey with the number 1,000 on it. The game continues half an hour later, but without him it has lost all interest. The crowd leaves the stands.

The next morning the Brazilian press divided its front pages equally between "Goal No. 1,000" and the landing on the moon of the astronauts Conrad and Bean.

But half of the other pages were devoted to the author of the most formidable series of goals ever scored by a soccer player. In every country public opinion honored the incredible feat.

For some weeks Pelé had to travel from stadium to stadium in Brazil to receive the homage of the crowds. Balls of solid gold, crowns, medals, laurels, honors of all sorts bestowed by civic and athletic authorities, perpetuated that memorable evening of November 19, 1969. At the entrance to Maracana Stadium a marble slab had already been fixed. Pelé would have to journey to the Alvorada Palace in Brasilia where the Head of State was organizing an official reception in his honor.

For several years "O Rei Pelé" (King Pelé) became a household word, and the news of "Goal No. 1,000" would spread across the world a title fully justified by the evidence.

In June 1970 the World Cup offered him an opportunity to show on the field how he bore the title bestowed on him.

The Mexican public had been won over to his cause in advance. But, as the experience in 1966 had shown, the pretenders to soccer supremacy were in a less conciliatory mood as the influence of money and the exigencies of national prestige offered increasing incitements to win at any price. Besides, the stormy resignation of Saldanha had left a good deal of disarray in the Brazilian camp.

Zagalo, the new technical director, lacked strength. He was ready to sacrifice the traditional offensive spirit of the Brazilian style in favor of the defensive conformity characteristic of European play.

Fortunately, Pelé had what his "technico" lacked. The two veterans Gerson and Carlos Alberto joined him, and the "triumvirate" had no trouble convincing Zagalo that Brazil should use a proven weapon rather than adopting the tactics of its opponents. Tostáo, disdained at first by the new selector, was confirmed in his role as starter at center forward. The style of play adopted would be offensive.

Right from its first moves in the Jalisco Stadium in Guadalajara, the Brazilian team demonstrated brilliantly that this choice was the right one. Against Czechoslovakia, Brazil created a sensation by displaying the kind of soccer that experienced observers of international matches had almost forgotten. Four admirable goals, magnificent team and individual moves, overcame the initial goal scored by the Czech forward Petras. Pelé scored a goal that will go down in soccer history, missed another by inches on a shot from 65 yards on a sudden inspiration, and put on a terrific show while simultaneously devoting himself to unselfish team play.

The deluge of praise for the "King," far from fostering his individual ego, reinforced his gifts as a team player. No longer the miracle player whose personal exploits "made the difference," he now placed all his strength at the service of his partners, doing his share of defending, feeding passes to build attacks, and giving up a shot for a pass when he judged it advantageous.

Against England, on the field of Guadalajara again, it took an incredible save by Banks, the English goalie, to push a cannon-like head shot by Pelé into the corner during a phase of the game when the Brazilians seemed as paralyzed by the fear of losing as their opponents. But with the score still 0–0 during the second half, Pelé received a goal-scoring pass from Tostao and made sure of the decisive goal by slipping the ball to Jairzinho with such a clever fake that the invincible Banks dived in vain.

In the victory over Rumania, Pelé personally contributed 2 goals which assured Brazil's qualification for the Quarter-finals. But in that game, against Peru, he let Tostao, Rivelino, and Jairzinho inscribe their names on the honor rolls of the "gole-adores." Life and soul of the team, he nonetheless played a decisive role in one of the most beautiful games in the whole competition—much to the regret of Didi, his former teammate, who had become the coach of the valorous "Inca" team, revelation of this World Cup.

The Semi-final against Uruguay posed a delicate psychological problem. The legendary tenacity of the players of the "Eastern Republic," plus their no less legendary roughness, had left a bitter memory for all Brazilians: the defeat incurred at Rio before 200,000 witnesses in the 1950 World Cup Final. Twenty years after that historic humiliation the successors of Ademir, Jair, and Zizinho still seemed traumatized by it, to judge by the initial 30 minutes of the game. Uruguay led 1–0 following a monumental error by Felix, the Brazilian goalkeeper, and their lead held up until only a few seconds were left in the first half. Pelé, closely checked, tackled hard by opponents who resorted to intimidation, was not much more brilliant than his teammates.

But everything changed from the moment Clodoaldo took the initiative by moving up on attack and received the pass from Tostao that enabled him to get the ball past Mazurkiewicz, the Uruguayan goalkeeper.

Despite violent fouls by Montero-Castillo and Mujica, Pelé and his teammates recovered their control. Jairzinho broke the tie after a beautiful Pelé-Tostao combination; and Pelé, after a royal breakaway, offered Rivelino the ball for an easy third goal.

In the final minutes he barely missed a fourth one after having completely befuddled the Uruguayan goalie with an extraordinary feint that made 70,000 spectators rise to their feet.

The road to the Final was clear. The partisans of "realistic" soccer believed that the air-tight defense of Italy and its specialists in counterattacks would unnerve the Brazilians, who would have to let down their guard in order to attack.

In meeting that type of opposition it is essential to strike early, and none was more apt to succeed in this than Pelé. In half an hour he had done the job by getting high up in the air and heading in a center from Rivelino. Despite an enormous error by the Brazilian defense, immediately exploited for a goal by Boninsegna, the South Americans had sized up their opponents. A superb shot by Gerson made it 2–1; then, twice in a row, Pelé, in favorable shooting position, slipped the ball to a partner—the first time to Jairzinho, the second to Carlos Alberto. On the electric scoreboard of Azteca Stadium was inscribed the triumph of a team that throughout the tournament had proved itself the incarnation of art in soccer.

Almost a billion TV viewers witnessed these soccer fireworks. A rain of confetti and paper streamers hurled down on the turf where Carlos Alberto, the "capitao," raised high the Jules Rimet Cup that was now the property of Brazil—the only nation to have captured it three times.

But the crowd yelled for Pelé. Never before had he given so many demonstrations of his genius as in this "Mundial," which he dominated completely.

For weeks Pelé and his teammates satisfied the invitations of his compatriots and then those of the Mexicans, where people could not applaud the "tricampeao" enough. Then Pelé revealed his decision not to participate in the 10th World Cup in Germany.

On June 18, 1971, just one year after the coronation at Azteca Stadium, he bade farewell to the team to which his destiny had been linked for fourteen years.

And on October 2, 1974, in the Villa Belmiro Stadium where,

in 1956, he had worn the white jersey with the emblem featuring the letters S.F.C. for the first time, he saluted his teammates and the spectators at the end of a game played against Ponte Preta.

Pelé had put an end to his career, just as he had said he would.

5

And He Set Out to Conquer the Stars . . .

On June 9, 1975, a brief news item appeared on the Telex machines of the international news agencies: Pelé had just signed a contract to play three seasons for the New York Cosmos, a club in the North American Soccer League which governs professional soccer in the United States. The conditions of the contract were revealed: Pelé would receive $7 million (of which $4.5 million reportedly would be tax-free) for wearing the colors of the New York club in eighty-five matches. He would also receive royalties on the profits of an advertising agency which would use his name in commercial advertising.

The signature of Steve Ross, president of Warner Communications—a powerful concern whose movie branch, Warner Bros., has been famous all over the world for half a century—guaranteed the execution of the most fabulous contract ever offered a soccer player. Warner Communications was indeed the owner of the New York Cosmos, having added to its multifarious activities the ownership and management of a soccer club.

The news created a sensation in international soccer circles where it was believed that F.C. Barcelona had established an unbeatable record by signing Cruyff for some $2 million. In the United States it was pointed out, with a good deal of amazement, that the salary for a top performer in soccer, considered a minor sport, was far superior to those of the highest paid stars in football, baseball, and basketball, including the famous Joe Namath and Abdul Jabar.

The news was better understood by those who were present two months before at the Van Himst Jubilee in Brussels, during which Pelé played on the same team with Cruyff, Eusebio, and other prestigious players invited to wear the colors of a world selection for the occasion. Despite abominable climatic conditions, Pelé showed the 30,000 spectators that he remained truly himself, the greatest of the great. The verdict of the "applause meter" when the teams were introduced proved that the popularity of Cruyff, prematurely labeled a "superstar," could not stand comparison with that of the conqueror of three World Cups.

The journalists present in Brussels knew that a special envoy from a New York club had been undertaking a regular siege of Pelé for some weeks, following him on all his trips with the avowed intention of obtaining his signature on a contract. But many remained skeptical about the American recruiter's chances of success. And when they learned that Pelé had signed the "contract of the century," it came as an enormous surprise.

In Brazil, where the news was announced in enormous headlines in all the papers, public opinion was at first divided. The official view was severe: Pelé had refused to play for the Brazilian team in the World Cup but accepted to play abroad for dollars. And Admiral Helio Nunes, the new president of the C.B.D., declared: "If Pelé plays in the United States, I shall recall him for the 1978 World Cup!"

Realistically, Brazilian public opinion on the whole showed more moderation: "In 1978 Pelé will be thirty-seven. . . . And then everybody is free to act the way he sees fit. . . ."

The most important Brazilian newspapers, at first reticent, soon openly showed their pride at the triumph scored by Pelé in his first return to action in the colors of the New York Cosmos—a white shirt with gold and green trimmings (the same as the Brazilian colors).

Among the 300 journalists who came to Downing Stadium on June 15, there were numerous special correspondents from the Rio and Sao Paulo papers. They were about to witness the most extraordinary comeback in soccer history.

From Europe came only three journalists: Norbet Eschmann, the former Swiss international forward; Roger Monnet, a photographer for *Miroir du Football*; and the author of this book, who did not want to miss the treat which a match by Pelé constitutes for soccer enthusiasts. But we also wanted to find out first-hand the reason for Pelé's change of mind eight months after he had announced his definite retirement.

After watching the three games Pelé played in the space of six days in New York (against Dallas and then against Toronto), and in Boston against the "Minutemen" led by Eusebio, these are the provisional conclusions I reached from my observations plus a rather lengthy talk with Pelé.

First the player. He remains in full possession of that genius which enables him to accomplish ever new and ever astounding creative moves. Physically, although his reflexes are a little slower, the solidity of his muscles and tendons—tested by three matches played in a very short space of time—has been reassuringly proved. His goal instinct and his appetite for victories, his intelligence in team play and his unselfishness are as evident as ever. And his personal effectiveness too, as shown by his splendid head goal against Dallas and his subsequent scores against Rochester, Boston (where his disallowed goal caused a near riot), and particularly Washington, where he set up 2 goals and tallied twice before a record crowd of 35,620, despite unusually difficult conditions.

His biggest problem is the weakness of most of his new teammates. In order to play alongside a player of Pelé's class, one must attain a technical level and a sense of team play that is sadly lacking in the majority of his partners. They are unable to foresee his intentions, collaborate in his initiatives, or execute with precision the technical actions called for.

The American public and press have fortunately displayed a

comprehension that is amazing for neophytes. While they showed their appreciation, by applause and enthusiastic comments, of Pelé's strokes of genius, while they were able, like Larry Merchant of the New York *Post*, to find the explanation for Pelé's triumphal debut in the U.S.A. in the fact that "he speaks a universal language," they also realized that the weakness of his partners limits his means of expression on the field.

But although this correct appraisal may induce Clive Toye, general manager of the Cosmos, to strengthen the roster of the club, it will not be because Pelé has insisted on it. On as well as off the field he acts toward his teammates like an older brother, solely concerned with aiding them for the good of the team, without ever showing the slightest impatience, irritation, or condescension.

When I questioned him about this, he replied with conviction:

"I am sure they will improve rapidly. They have qualities and they will succeed in expressing them. When I accepted the task I've been entrusted with, I did so fully aware of what it involved, without the slightest illusion about the difficulties I would have to face, for here you have to start from scratch. You've seen their pitches, they're not soccer fields. As for facilities, they're worlds behind those of the European or South American clubs. No technical personnel, no trainers, no club physician, no one in charge of equipment. For the first time since 1956, since my early days as a professional player, I've had to clean my soccer shoes myself. But . . . it's tremendous, because people are counting on me to win over a country of 200 million inhabitants who had viewed soccer with hostility. And I didn't accept that responsibility only for the money. I did so because it represents an exciting challenge, too."

Hasn't Pelé been signed to play soccer? Of course. But not merely to play soccer. Steve Ross, president of Warner Communications, did not budget $7 million just to satisfy a show-biz tycoon's whim. And the belief that he has made a profitable investment is not just based on the anticipated receipts of the New

York Cosmos. He is gambling on a far larger scale. He and his firm are engaged in a vast long-term project: to establish soccer in the United States, professional soccer of course, but also the amateur soccer which is an indispensable basis for its success.

Profiting from the negative experience of previous costly attempts, which tried to appeal to recent European immigrants who were interested only in watching players from their native countries, Warner decided on another course: to win over the great American public, which had been prejudiced toward a sport that the organizers wanted to impose on it via small ethnic groups.

How could this be done? By signing up the man who was the indisputable image of the art of soccer, but the man too who, in the eyes of the world, embodied a sport endowed with a universal audience.

That is why they gave preference to a Black player of thirty-four, whose worldwide popularity illustrates so well the universality of soccer, over players at the height of their career such as Cruyff, Beckenbauer, or Edstroem. Warner figured, and rightly so, that only the magnetism of "locomotive" Pelé's name was strong enough to draw American youth into the soccer stadiums.

The initial success exceeded all hopes. "Pelé's Triumphant Debut: U.S. Soccer Finds a Saviour," read the cover page of *Sports Illustrated*, which featured, for the first time in this important magazine's existence, the star of a sport recently considered minor. Pelé's first game, televised live by CBS, pulled a 5.1 rating nationally and 10.3 in New York. These ratings are all the more impressive because a competing network was simultaneously televising a program about the French Tennis Internationals which was a complete fiasco in the ratings—and one that could not be explained solely by the heat which drew New Yorkers to the beaches.

For the first time, too, the press devoted headlines and large space on the inner pages to soccer, which it had previously ignored almost completely. Considering the near monopoly baseball holds in the sports pages during the summer months, this is some measure of the effectiveness of Pelé's name in the field of soccer promotion.

Now that a breach has been created in the American sports tradition, can it be enlarged? Soccer still has to overcome some severe obstacles.

The first lies in the absence of a material base: playing fields for amateurs, big stadiums for professionals. A difficult problem in large towns where real-estate speculations come first, as always, and where established sports jealously keep their facilities to themselves. The dearth of competent, experienced technical staff falls obviously under the same heading.

The second obstacle is the awesome competition of the big American sports. You only have to switch on the television to realize the importance of baseball, an integral part of the famous "American way of life." Basketball, a sport born in the U.S.A. and exported to the rest of the world, has remained so popular that, to see a professional game in Madison Square Garden, one has to buy a season ticket. Above all, there is the competition posed by American football, which has a relatively short season (four months) but fills 100,000-seat stadiums and has no intention of collaborating in the establishment of a rival sport.

Nevertheless, Pelé and the pioneers of soccer in the United States are optimistic. One reason, which struck the most clear-sighted observers of the New York press particularly, is the impact Pelé's arrival on the scene has created on adults who recognize him in the street and ask for his autograph, and especially on the young and very young. One only had to see the enraptured looks of the ball-boys who formed a hedge for his entry on the turf of Downing Stadium or of Nickerson Field in Boston to understand that in this essential area, since it involves the future of soccer, the enterprise has had a marvelous beginning.

The NASL got the message so well that henceforth before each professional match a preliminary game features two kids' or junior teams which the spectators, most of whom are young, always follow with great interest.

Certain newspapers, for example the New York *Daily News*,

devote daily columns to explanations and commentaries on the laws of soccer, as well as elementary methods of teaching soccer techniques and tactics.

This development is no doubt due to Pelé, whose name appears constantly in newspaper columns and on the air—to his genius as a soccer player but also to the power of his personality, which inspires respect and liking. However, among the factors contributing to this development one cannot ignore the change in social climate that immediately strikes a foreigner returning to New York for the first time after thirteen years. This change is expressed by the questioning of many earlier prejudices and preconceived ideas, of which the indifference toward soccer, an immigrant sport, was one.

New York Cosmos . . . In 1974 the name could be considered very ambitious. Since Pelé's arrival the conquest of the stars—national emblem for the states which make up one of the most powerful nations in the world—is perhaps within reach of the number one leader in the world of soccer.

And if soccer succeeds in conquering the last country that has refused to become part of its empire, Pelé will have achieved his greatest feat.

PART TWO

The Artist

In every country the passion of crowds for soccer—top sport in the 141 nations grouped under the blue flag of the International Federation (FIFA)—crystallizes around the names of those players whose talent or genius has won their admiration.

Despite the existence of competitions such as the World Cup, and the Cups of Europe, South America, Africa, Central America, and Southeast Asia, it is rare for these names to be universally acknowledged outside the continents where they achieved their fame.

Alfredo Di Stefano, undisputed number one player in Europe during the period when Real piled up victories in every stadium of the Old World, has never been recognized in South America or even in his native Argentina. In Buenos Aires, thirty years after their retirement from active play, people talk with admiration of Jose Manuel Moreno, Adolfo Pedernera, even of Arsenio Erico (despite his Paraguayan nationality), but not of Di Stefano, even though, during his Argentine career, the fans gave him the flattering nickname of "Saeta Rubia" (the Blond Arrow).

In spite of the prestige he obtained as captain of the unforgettable 1953 Hungarian team and later with the great Real Madrid, Ferenc Puskas has never been appreciated as he deserves *on the other side of the Atlantic, because circumstances limited him to brief appearances there.*

The names of Just Fontaine—whose record 13 goals scored in the 1958 World Cup have not been equaled—and of Raymond Kopa are known in Rio de Janeiro and in Buenos Aires, but the two most famous players in the history of French soccer have had only a few occasions to give concrete proof of their vast abilities to the spectators of these capitals of South American soccer.

But mention the name of Pelé in the most distant and backward regions of the globe and you will notice that it evokes an amazingly precise image as well as affection and admiration in all.

Pelé People rally unanimously round those two syllables. In the eyes of the world, Soccer is Pelé!

6

The Masterpieces

In the museum at Ipiranga in south central Paraná, a gigantic blow-up 33 feet wide shows Pelé in the white jersey of Santos heading the ball into an empty goal as four players in dark shirts look on in consternation. One of them, the goalkeeper, is on the ground, and the position of his body forces him to turn his head to contemplate the image of his defeat.

This photo captures what Pelé long considered his most beautiful goal, an opinion shared by those who witnessed this scene and then decided to immortalize it in this monumental form.

The scene was the small stadium of Juventus, one of those poor professional clubs that live in the shadow of the famous teams of the Paulista League and limit their ambitions to giving them a rough time when playing at home.

On August 2, 1959, the game against Santos in the small arena of the Rua Javari had attracted an excited crowd eager to watch two players who had been crowned world champions a year before in Stockholm, and determined to show them no indulgence.

Right from kickoff the most aggressive supporters of the local team had picked Pelé as their target.

When his first shot hit the outside of the net, a powerful voice, accompanied by ironic laughs and booing, shouted:

"Hey, 'negrinho' [little nigger], you're nothing but an apprentice."

A few moments later Pelé's pass to his left wing Pepé was too short. Now insults hurled down on him:

"Pailhaço [clown], go back to Bauru. Your place is in the forest."

Pelé headed a ball over the crossbar. From the same stands came a volley of insults:

"Macao! Forget soccer, it's not a game for niggers!"

Now Pelé was at mid-field, controlling the ball with his chest. An opponent flung himself at him; he avoided him by backing up and, before the ball touched the ground, lifted it over the head of his attacker, took it on his foot in full stride, eliminated a second defender in the same way, then a third, and finally the goalie who had come out to challenge him. Then he flicked the ball into the empty net, this time with his head.

The crowd could hardly believe its eyes. Pelé had juggled the ball over a distance of 50 yards while thwarting the furious assaults of four adversaries and flipping it into the goal with an ease that bordered on the miraculous. Four "chapeus" in an irresistible obstacle race. Nobody believed such a technical feat was possible!

Pelé did not stop to look at the ball deep in the net while the crowd roared its enthusiasm. He ran toward the stands whence came the insults and screamed:

"That's how monkeys score goals!"

Just for good measure, he added 2 more and Juventus was beaten 4–0.

Did he ever achieve a comparable individual feat again?

The 100,000 spectators of the Brazilian Cup match between Santos and Fluminense on March 5, 1961, at Maracana Stadium thought so.

On that day the "torcedores" (supporters) of Fluminense were not unhappy with the turn of events. Their favorites, thanks to a very tight defense, were holding Santos in check. With 15 minutes to go in regulation time the score was 1–1, and Castilho,

the excellent international goalie, noticed with satisfaction that
Pelé was operating way in the back, even very close to Laercio,
the "portier" of Santos.

He was not particularly concerned when Pelé took the ball in
that area, nor when he got by two Fluminense players. In order
to become a real threat, Pelé would still have to cross some 80
yards. What happened next left the large crowd stupefied. Faking repeated passes, Pelé dribbled past all the opponents he met
on his way until only Castilho was left, and then placed the ball
in a corner of the Fluminense goal despite a desperate dive by his
last opponent.

Here too Pelé seems to have exceeded the bounds of the possible by carrying an inconceivable undertaking to a successful
conclusion: scoring a goal by dribbling past the players of an
entire team renowned for its fighting spirit and its solid defense
as if it were child's play.

That day a picturesque expression was coined to describe a
goal which requires uncommon qualities in the way it is scored:
"Gol de placa" (a plaque goal). And indeed, to commemorate
that unforgettable goal, the Carioca Federation decided to put
up a plaque in the stadium where it was accomplished. A second
plaque would later appear within those same walls to recall that
it was the scene of Pelé's 1,000th goal.

I myself did not witness the two masterpieces just described,
although I have faithfully summarized the reports that appeared
in the Brazilian press at that time.

But as early as 1958 in Stockholm, the Semi-final and Final
of the World Cup convinced me immediately that the dark-
skinned adolescent who had scored 3 goals against France and 2
against Sweden was endowed with incomparable qualities.

In my report of the match between France and Brazil, published in *Miroir-Sprint*, I wrote under the headline "Three Head
Shots by Tremendous Pelé":

Three times Pelé, the young 17-year-old Black marvel, triumphed
over stubborn resistance by the French defense faced with a super-

human task. The first was scored by converting a center from Vava point-blank. The second after a splendid combination with Garrincha and Vava. The third following a long, high pass which he controlled in full movement before scoring with a masterful shot.

These lines are taken from my report of the Final between Brazil and Sweden:

It was Pelé, the 17-year-old "phenomenon," who ensured the victory of his team with an extraordinary third goal. At the 55th minute of the game, the calm Nilton Santos sends him the long pass he had called for. He calmly chest-controls the ball, lobs it over the head of Gustavsson and volleys it goal-bound before it touches the ground. The shot ends up deep in the net.

If we recall that he had begun his career in that very World Cup (against Wales) with an identical goal, it is perhaps less surprising that, spurred by both self-confidence and anger, he was able, in the Juventus game, to multiply fourfold a feat he knew so well.

An opponent's reputation is not the sort of obstacle to stop Pelé, nor is the importance of what is at stake.

In September 1962, Santos, which had carried off the South American Cup for the first time, played for the Intercontinental Final against Benfica, who were the crowned European champions following a somewhat lucky victory over Barcelona. In this home-and-home series, Santos eked out a 3–2 victory in the first leg at Maracana Stadium. Pelé scored 2 of his team's goals. But it was too small a lead in this type of competition. The Portuguese, who had profited by experience (the previous year they were badly beaten in Montevideo after having won in Lisbon), had no doubt that they would overcome the one-goal handicap and defeat Santos—with the help of 70,000 fans, who would support them in their stronghold, the Estadio da Luz.

They had confidence in the effectiveness of Eusebio, a rising star; in the skill of Coluna and Santana; and especially in their solid defense, set up by their coach Riera. But they had forgotten one thing: the presence of Pelé in the Santos line-up.

The result of the match: 5–0 with 13 minutes to go, 5–2 at the final whistle and Santos was world champion of clubs.

Pierre Lameignère, special correspondent of *Miroir-Sprint* in Lisbon, described the incredible rout of Benfica in these terms: "The evidence was unmistakable. Pelé played an exceptional role in this game. He scored three goals, two of which were the result of astounding individual exploits. In scoring the other two goals he supplied the decisive pass after irresistible dribbles."

Here is a detailed account of two moments in Pelé's performance:

At 45 yards from Costa-Pereira, the Portuguese goalie Zito intercepts a pass and immediately sends the ball to Pelé who is challenged by Cavem. A feint . . . no more Cavem. Two more amazing dribbles and Raul, followed by Humberto, suffer the same fate. The shot from 11 yards ends up in the net. . . .

A little later Pelé, in wing position, receives a pass from Lima. He dribbles around Cruz and then Raul, and from the touchline centers back to Coutinho who only has to push the ball into the goal.

The title of Pierre Lameignère's article is revealing: "Pelé's Instinctive Genius Makes a World Champion of Santos."

As the special correspondent of *Miroir-Sprint* in Lisbon made clear, Pelé's genius was also demonstrated in the creation of two moves that led to goals by his teammates Coutinho and Pepé.

This is nothing new. Up to now I have stressed the goals Pelé scored himself, because they constitute a spectacular proof of the value of an attacker, and their number is significant. Moreover, they offer valuable insights into the development of his career by enabling us to measure the fluctuations in his effectiveness and to note a certain change in his style of play.

But it must be pointed out that Pelé was never an individualist on the field and, while he scored goals, he always repaid his teammates by offering them innumerable chances to beat opposing goalkeepers.

I myself witnessed something very significant on June 1, 1961, at the Saint-Jacques Stadium in Basel. That evening Santos inflicted a crushing defeat (8–3) on the local team, one of the best in Switzerland and reinforced for the occasion by three international players. Of the 8 Brazilian goals, 5 were credited to Coutinho and 3 to Pelé.

The Santos team had been quite disappointing in its preceding matches, played without Pelé, who had been detained in Brazil due to the aftereffects of an injury.

But the day before the game the Swiss organizers received good news which they hastily relayed to the public by superimposing a line in enormous letters on the posters:

"PELÉ KOMMT UND SPIELT!" (PELÉ COMES AND PLAYS.) That changed everything, of course; most of all the gate.

The spectators will long remember the spectacle they watched that evening. Was it the joy of being with his teammates again? Or the pleasure of practicing his art once more after several weeks of being laid up? In any case, Pelé, like Prometheus unbound, displayed such imagination in his feints, his dribbles, and passes that the unfortunate Swiss player charged with defending him spent most of the evening lunging into empty space. Nevertheless, the sports fans, who are sometimes cruel, did not have the heart to laugh at the useless efforts, the blind determination, the confusion of this befuddled defender. Who could have stopped this black demon who popped up all along the Swiss defense and got by it with such ridiculous ease?

Of the 3 goals he scored himself, 2 remain engraved on my memory:

As he is moving the ball, a Swiss fullback comes at him full speed and tries to get him off balance with a shoulder charge. But Pelé, in full motion, pivots around like a spinning top, avoids contact, and ends up all alone with the ball in front of the Swiss goalie.

A few minutes later, two opponents come right at him. A

body feint, they give way as if pulled by invisible hands, Pelé moves into the opening, avoids the charge of a third opponent by a sudden change of pace, calmly eliminates the goalie by a change of direction, and pushes the ball into the empty goal.

But these personal exploits give only an imperfect idea of his amazing performance. Of the 5 goals scored by his "student" Coutinho, 3 were gifts from the "master," whose genius revealed itself as briiliantly in their conception as the execution.

Pelé-Coutinho: the two names will long be linked in the memories of the crowds who witnessed the soccer festivals during the Paris Tournaments of the sixties. From them students of the game learned the meaning of the word "tabelha," and the effectiveness of the maneuver known in English as the "wall pass" or the "give-and-go" when executed by virtuosi in curved passes.

The "tabelha" enabled Santos to unbalance the excellent defenses of Reims and Racing Paris in a series of collective moves of extraordinary purity.

During one of those evenings still remembered with nostalgia in Parisian soccer circles, Pelé and Coutinho showed how perfect their understanding was, even when one of them suddenly decided to vary an expected move.

They had just advanced with a series of wall passes that had thrown panic into the Racing defense when suddenly Pelé, who had slipped the ball to Coutinho for a return pass, abruptly changed the usual direction of his forward motion and instead headed full speed toward Coutinho. The latter, instead of making the return pass, let the ball go past him so that Pelé could recover it without opposition, since the Parisian defenders had been completely pulled out of position by the brilliant improvisation of the two Brazilians. It is one of the finest examples of instantaneous comprehension that can be used to illustrate what collective intelligence in soccer is all about.

In the 1966 World Cup Pelé really played only one match—at Liverpool against Bulgaria—since he started the game against Portugal still hampered by the injury received from Jetchev and was rapidly "finished off" by Morais.

Most people only remember the aggressions committed against him. Personally, I have not forgotten two of his exploits in the game against Bulgaria which he performed in spite of the brutalities and the unmerciful attack to which he was subjected for the full 90 minutes. His goal scored on a free kick with a powerful shot from 25 yards out seemed like poetic justice, all the more so since he had been the victim of a tripping foul by Yakimov.

But for a player of his class that was not a remarkable feat. The two actions I am going to try to describe were worthy of inclusion in the classics of soccer.

The first takes place right on the edge of the touchline in mid-field. In order to receive a pass from his right fullback, Pelé suddenly moves backward, followed as if he were his shadow by Jetchev.

When the ball gets to him, a hard pass chest-high, Pelé is less than 2 feet from the touchline facing his own goal. He controls the ball with his chest, starting a body movement that makes Jetchev think he will try to move off perpendicular to the touchline. The Bulgarian takes off in that direction. But it was a feint. Pelé bends down slightly, the ball passes over his left shoulder, he recovers it flush on the touchline by pivoting on his right foot, and moves off at top speed. In just a few seconds he has faked the pants off his opponent and created space in the narrow corridor his feint had opened up. What imagination, what technical perfection in a totally unexpected move!

Now to the second feat. The entire Bulgarian team is massed in front of its penalty area. On the left side of the field Pelé takes a flat pass. He makes as if to move on a slant directly into the crowded center. But he abruptly changes direction and runs parallel to the Bulgarian goal. One, two, three, four opponents come at him to get the ball. He eliminates them at full speed, manages to move around the penalty area on the right, goes forward on the side, moves in and, from 11 yards, lets go a terrific cross shot which the Bulgarian goalie just manages to deflect into the corner. A race—ball at his feet—of more than 70 yards

strewn with fearful obstacles, terminated by such a cannon shot
. . . that is an athletic performance that pushes back the limits of
what we consider possible.

Nonetheless, at the time certain critics did not hesitate to say
that his injuries had masked the sad reality of his decline. For the
sake of their reputation it is to be hoped that they were not
present at this game between Brazil and Bulgaria. Four years
later, in the 1970 World Cup, they would have had no choice but
to admit that their judgment had been wildly premature.

7

The Team Player

The enormous repercussions of the 1,000th goal, scored seven months before the 70 "Mundial," undoubtedly contributed powerfully to restoring Pelé's original hallmark. In the eyes of the vast majority of sports fans throughout the world, he is the man who scores goals practically at will, because he possesses a gift that some would not hesitate to call supernatural.

It must be admitted that appearances can be disturbing. The Parisian soccer spectators can confirm this. In 1963, during a catastrophic tour in Europe (suffering a sensational 5–1 loss to Belgium), the Brazilian team faced France at Colombes Stadium. The visitors created the same bad impression as in other games in the Old World. But in this game they had Pelé, who had been unable to play the preceding matches. Pelé, still hampered by an injury, was not in great form; far from it. But Brazil finally savored victory: 3–2. Three goals by Pelé!

In Brazil they tell of an even more significant event. It took place during a Semi-final of the Brazilian Cup in 1964, between Santos and Gremio de Porto Alegre in Pacaembu Stadium at Sao Paulo.

Santos had been ahead 1–0 since early in the game and seemed to be heading for an easy victory. With a quarter of an hour left to play, Gremio tied and in a few minutes went ahead 3–1. An angry reaction by Santos resulted in a goal, then the tie, and finally 4–3. Three goals by Pelé had reversed the situation!

But it was not over yet. In the heat of this sensational ending Gilmar, the international goalie for Santos, argued with the referee and was sent off the field. Who took his place in the goal? Pelé, who made two extraordinary saves on point-blank shots by Gremio forwards and protected a victory that may well be called his own.

This "superman" image was, however, badly tarnished by his muscular accident in Vina del Mar in 1962, by the knee injury in Liverpool in 1966, and by the period of discouragement that followed.

But if he proved, quite involuntarily, that he is not immune from physical and moral problems, in Mexican stadiums throughout the Mundial before the largest public ever to watch a sports event (1 billion TV viewers), Pelé demonstrated that voluntary integration in the team is a necessary condition for the full flowering of a soccer player's genius.

Sure enough, in the six matches played and won by Brazil he used that "scoring instinct" which no one has ever possessed in such highly developed form—but only when there was no other choice to be certain of victory.

In the game against Czechoslovakia, the score was 1–1, and the opponent was threatening when Pelé attempted an apparently senseless shot at goal from 65 yards out. The initial reaction from 80,000 spectators was: "He's crazy! No, it's a stroke of genius!" There followed a huge ovation from the crowd on its feet in the stands. Through the curtain of opponents and partners, Pelé alone in the entire stadium at Guadalajara had spotted the advanced position of Viktor, the Czech goalie, whereupon he instantaneously decided on and executed the necessary lob shot.

But because he missed the distant target by inches, he had to draw closer to it, since the go-ahead goal was needed. Seeing his lightning start from right-wing position, Gerson, understanding his maneuver, sent him a long, lifted pass. The trajectory of the ball was very high. Anyone but Pelé would have been forced to head it. But he, rising high in the air, used his chest to control the ball, at the same time turning 180° to protect it against a de-

Born to play ball (Stockholm 1958, on the eve of the World Cup Semi-Final Brazil-France).

World champion at seventeen, surrounded by his teammates of the 1958 B[...]
team. (Back row, l. to r.): D. Santos, Zito, Bellini, N. Santos, Gilmar. (Fro[...]
l. to r.): Garrincha, Didi, Pelé, Vava, Zagalo.

Soldier at the Santos garrison

The "goal man" (the "gol de placa" of March 5, 1961).

The "Goal No. 1,000" of November 19, 1969.

The injured player of Vina del Mar (1962 World Cup).

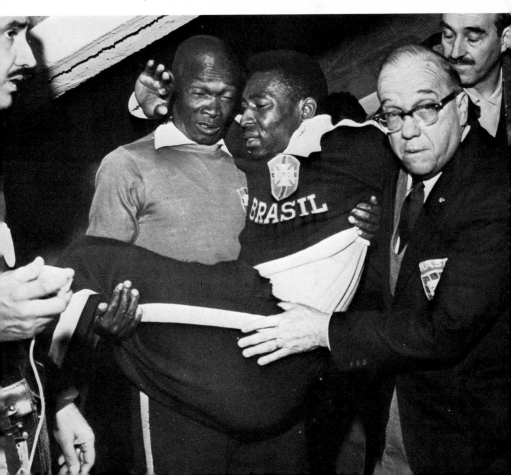

The return to life (the "bicicletta," Maracana, 1963).

The target of violence (Liverpool, 1966, and Mexico City, 1970).

Santos: si! World Cup: no! (Santos, 1968).

World Cup? Si! (Guadalajara, 1970).

Strike the first! (the first goal of the 1970 Final at Mexico City).

Letting a teammate have the last word...(the last goal of the 1970 Final).

The man in the team (Mexico City 1970, Brazilian tea
Back row (l. to r.): Carlos Alberto, Felix, Piazza, Br
Clodoaldo, Everaldo. Front row (l. to r.): Jairzinho, Gers
Tostao, Pelé, Rivelino.

His third World Cup (Mexico City,
).

Above: Good-bye to the national
team (Rio de Janeiro, July 18, 1971).

What is a feint? (Guadalajara, 1970, Pelé and Mazurkiewicz).

Pelé begins his career in New York with the Cosmos.

fender who was guarding him closely, then let it slide down his body, looked up to check the position of Viktor who had come out to narrow the shooting angle, and dispatched a violent, right-footed shot that made the net bulge. This masterpiece of technical execution, accomplished in a few seconds, had a decisive influence on the outcome of the game, which Brazil finally won 4–1.

Against England, Pelé rapidly sensed that his team, fear-ridden by the memory of its setback in the 1966 World Cup and by the absence of Gerson, one of its "brains," needed to become conscious of its strengths. On a high center from Jairzinho, he drove in from the position of the classical center forward, and his head shot, "angled" toward one of the corners of the goal, would have beaten any goalkeeper other than the astounding Gordon Banks. We shall see later how he finally brought the English goalie to his knees.

In the Final against Italy, Pelé knew that it was vital for Brazil to score the first goal in order to oblige the opponent (who operated by counterattacks based on a reinforced defense) to open up its guard.

As in the game with England, he suddenly appeared in the position of center forward, where he changed the trajectory of a slowly descending pass from Rivelino by rising with an impressive jump above the solid Burgnich to catapult the ball with his head into the net past goalie Albertosi.

This exploit would have an important psychological bearing on the final 4–1 victory which gave Brazil its third World Cup trophy.

Except for the goal he put in against Czechoslovakia, none of the others Pelé scored in the 1970 Mundial in Mexico can be included among his most spectacular tallies, even if their tactical importance was capital. His modest total of 4 goals for the entire tournament was, moreover, far less than that of his teammate Jairzinho (7) and the German forward Gerd Muller (10).

But it was evident from the first game by Brazil at Guadalajara that Pelé was not after the record established by Fontaine in Sweden (13 goals) but the conquest of the World Cup by his team. His contribution as a team player proved immediately to be more important than it had been in the past.

Certainly all those who had admired the marvelous "tabelhas" between Pelé and Coutinho knew to what extent Pelé possesses the intelligence of team play; but not having seen him often enough in action, they were unaware of the full scope of his repertory in the creation of team movements.

Beginning with the match between Brazil and Czechoslovakia—one of those encounters of which it can justly be said that they are unforgettable—the evidence was unmistakable. Operating most frequently in a less advanced position than before, Pelé's action was more sustained than in the past, and he exerted a decisive influence on his partners. It is true that, starting from far back, he often attempted incursions by dribbling or the "give-and-go" passes that make opposing defenders panic. But he frequently played in the manner of a mid-fielder, starting the movement of the ball by lateral passes or participating in it by return passes either as the pivot or as back-up player. His participation in defensive tasks was usually limited to acting as "screen," which facilitates interception of passes by a partner. But at times he could be seen tackling like a fullback when there was need for it.

A born attacker, it is of course in the advanced positions where he manages to turn up at the opportune moment and that he accomplishes the decisive actions that place a partner in ideal scoring position.

In the game against England, Banks expected Pelé to shoot and closed the angle when the latter received a pass from Tóstao 6 yards in front of the goal. But a short pass putting the ball at the feet of the onrushing Jairzinho left the goal wide open for an unstoppable shot.

Against Peru, on a pass by Jairzinho, Pelé was in position to beat the goalie. Even though Brazil was leading, he chose to make sure by slipping the ball to Tostao who was in a still more favorable position.

As against Peru, he did not register any goal in the Semi-final against Uruguay. But he made up for that by offering Rivelino the opportunity to fire off one of those bullets for which the mustachioed Brazilian is famous. Pelé, in possession of the ball, had driven deep into the Uruguayan defense and by the time he got to the edge of the penalty area, only one defender was left to be passed. To the crowd's amazement he came to a sudden stop. He had sensed that Rivelino was following him, so he pushed the ball scarcely 2 yards in front of the left foot of his teammate, who was moving at top speed. Mazurkiewicz, the excellent Uruguayan keeper, had to get the ball out of the back of the net.

He would have been even unhappier if, a few moments later, after he had come out to intercept a long pass by a Brazilian defender and Pelé had completely befuddled him by an extraordinary body feint, he had conceded a fourth goal. Fortunately for the ego of this remarkable goalie, the rapid arrival of his teammate Ancheta forced Pelé to cross his shot and the ball grazed the post on the wrong side. All this time Mazurkiewicz was lying on the ground, 20 yards in front of his goal. The crowd in Guadalajara is not likely to forget this "genialidad" which made it rise to its feet.

As mentioned above, Pelé got even for this in the Final— much to the woe of the Italian goalie Albertosi. He even collected interest since, in addition to the decisive goal he scored early in the game, he made two assists in the second half which were so well timed and accurate that Jairzinho and later Carlos Alberto only had to hit the ball hard in the direction they were moving in order to have their names figure, alongside Pelé's and Gerson's, on the glorious list of "goleadores" of a "historic" match. Historic because for the first time a team had won its third World Cup. Historic because for the first time a player had accomplished the same feat. Historic because it marked the triumph of offensive, constructive, artistic soccer over a conception of the sport characterized by the belief in winning by any means, including the most sordid.

8

In a Class by Himself

The birth of the Fédération Internationale de Football Association (FIFA) in 1904 was the official proclamation of the universality of soccer. But only in 1930 did the FIFA assert itself in action for the first time in the form of the single competition open to all nations: the World Cup.

It is useless to attempt comparisons between clubs and players whose active careers took place before with those who came after that date, since there can be no objective judgments.

So, too, it is difficult to measure the respective worth of the three generations of players that have followed each other since the first World Cup. The Italians Meazza and Ferrari, who were twice on the championship team before the Second World War, were certainly two of the great forwards of their time. But the progress accomplished since 1945 in the fields of individual technique, physical conditioning, and tactics have placed their successors in infinitely more difficult playing conditions. The numerical reinforcement of defenses, and particularly the unscrupulous means used by defenders to stop opponents, require of the forwards much greater speed in conception and execution and a much greater physical resistance, not to mention the indispensable courage to take serious risks.

However skillful, however astute the great prewar players may have been—Meazza, Ferrari, Sindelar, Sarosi, Alec James,

Leonidas, whom I had the opportunity to see in action—one cannot be sure that they would have been equally brilliant if they had been born twenty years later.

The same reservation must be made for the great forwards who shone during the golden age of soccer in Argentina, spared the horrors of the war—Jose Manuel Moreno, Adolfo Pedernera, Walter Gomez, Barnabe Ferreyra—men whose names are still pronounced with respect all over South America.

On the other hand, there is nothing to prevent us from comparing the players who have delighted fans in stadiums all over the world from 1952 until the present. Provided, that is, we do not forget that the toughening of defensive play has increased with the years, posing ever greater problems for attackers, the true soccer artists.

It is from this perspective that we must examine the unanimous decision that Pelé is the greatest soccer player of all time.

His medals and titles alone (in athletics they have real meaning) would suffice to prove that the popular judgment is founded on good evidence. No one had ever won three World Cups, or scored 1,000 goals in top competition, before Pelé.

The Brazilians Gilmar, Garrincha, Nilton and Djalma Santos, Zito, Didi, and Zagalo all captured two World Cups in a four-year interval. Their soccer career was well over when Pelé conquered his third title, twelve years after his first. The splendor of Pelé's international career is only matched by its exceptional length.

Among the famous postwar attackers who retired shortly before or after Pelé conquered his first world title, some sported a World Cup victory: the German Fritz Walter and the Uruguayan Juan Schiaffino. But the Hungarians Puskas and Hidegkuti, the French players Kopa and Fontaine, the Hispano-Argentine Di Stefano have never known this honor.

Di Stefano, the most prestigious name on this list, would have appeared in the final round of the '62 Mundial in Chile if an unfortunate injury had not kept him out of the Spanish selection.

The case of this lord in the realm of the round ball, conqueror five times in succession of the European Cup and deprived of the chance to distinguish himself in the greatest competition of his sport, illustrates the dependence of a soccer player on his team and on other circumstances affecting his career. However great his individual merit may be, a player can prove it in competition only to the extent that his team also participates brilliantly. Since Argentina forfeited in 1950 and Spain did not get past the elimination rounds in 1954 and 1958, Di Stefano cannot compete in the World Cup. In 1962 he missed his chance because he had no choice.

Everybody remembers the enormous misfortune of Puskas, the best attacker of the years 1953–54, who fell at the head of the great Hungarian team in the World Cup Final at Bern after having temporarily been sidelined, due to an aggression by one of those who were to be his conquerors. This defeat did not prevent Puskas from enjoying an illustrious career later on, by strange coincidence in company with Di Stefano and Kopa—two men who had not been able to capture the World Cup.

Nevertheless it remains true—in view of the quality of Brazilian soccer as attested by the participation of its team in all ten World Cups—that three wins in a competition which is only held once every four years is a feat not likely to be equaled before the year 2000.

Although no player can boast of possessing titles that compare with those of Pelé, nonetheless interesting comparisons are possible when one has seen all the great players of the past thirty years in action, as I have been fortunate enough to do.

One of the greatest forwards I have known was the Uruguayan Juan Schiaffino, that jewel of soccer players who enabled the team of his little country to accomplish one of the most prodigious exploits in the history of soccer, beating Brazil and seizing the World Cup from it in 1950 before 200,000 Brazilians convinced of the superiority of their team. Schiaffino was the complete forward, capable of tilting the game by a goal scored after a 70-yard run, but also of brilliant passes, and of fighting with enormous determination. What a pity that he never played against or on the same team with Pelé. I shall never forget the feats he accomplished in that memorable Semi-Final between Hungary and Uruguay in the 1954 World Cup.

During the most brilliant period of his career (1952–62), Di Stefano combined his effectiveness as a goal scorer—five times number one "goleador" of the Spanish championship games, he remains the top scorer in the history of the European Cup—with the ceaseless activity, tactical intelligence, and technical mastery of a great strategist.

This tall, powerful athlete had the bearing of a lord of the stadiums nothing could stop. A great sports adventurer, he had gone through the heroic era of the Colombian outlaws after the long strike of the Argentine professional players in 1949. Later on he was even kidnapped by terrorists in Venezuela, a mishap he took very philosophically. His most vicious opponents never dared use rough tactics against this Jupiter who would have smitten them with his gaze. His partners accepted unquestioningly the rule of an uncontested leader who gave generously of himself.

Di Stefano was the incarnation of Real Madrid, whose glorious period began when he got off the plane from Bogota and which became just another team the day he decided to "hang up his shoes." He was its soul and its all-around player, the one who by voice and gesture directed the energies of his partners, the one who defended, constructed, and tallied.

Talented from top to toe, all-knowing, all over the field, an unconquerable fighter, what was lacking in this player, who will remain one of the greats in soccer history, was the spark of genius. Di Stefano always did exactly what had to be done. But I never saw him do what Pelé does in no matter what game: conceive and execute something that nobody else had imagined. *Creation* in the true sense of the word.

Ferenc Puskas did possess genius. Right from his arrival at Real Madrid when everybody considered him "finished," that was probably what earned him the respect of Di Stefano, then at the height of his fame. He had proved it as captain of the Hungarian team which, in Wembley Stadium, had ground to dust the myth of the supremacy of English soccer on its own soil; and in the 1954 World Cup, which had ended with the greatest denial of justice in the history of sports. He proved it again with Real Madrid, notably in that unforgettable 1960 European Cup Final when he registered 4 of the 7 goals in the crushing victory of Real Madrid over Eintracht Frankfurt.

Puskas had intuition and marvelous surprise moves—and a left foot he could use like a hand for cannon shots and completely unpredictable passes. But he possessed neither the speed, the "spring," nor the necessary resistance to accomplish what Pelé conceives and executes apparently without effort.

With a more complete technical mastery, a less fanciful humor, an intelligence on the field that sometimes bordered on genius, Nandor Hidegkuti, Puskas's companion in the changing fortunes of the great Hungarian team, was also one of the players whose names will remain in the annals of international soccer. Skillful in constructing, excellent in the finish, he too did not possess the mobility, the muscular spurt, the fertile imagination that would permit comparison with Pelé.

Two French forwards, Raymond Kopa and Just Fontaine, have had the distinguished honor of being preferred to Pelé during the 1958 World Cup. The former was named most valuable player of the competition by the international press. The latter was clearly ahead of the Brazilian in the standings of goal scorers, setting a record unequaled to this day (13 goals in the final round). But with a clear-sightedness that does them credit, the two great players acknowledged even then the exceptional qualities of the young Pelé.

A magnificent dribbler and feinter, an effective scorer in spite of appearances (the statistics prove it), often a genius in the conception of the decisive pass, an indefatigable athlete and true sparkplug of the team, Kopa has always been an admirer of the player who was his fortunate rival in Stockholm.

In a very different style from Pelé's, Fontaine showed an exceptional goal instinct that went ideally with Kopa's constructive play and a rather rare intelligence of movement. His premature retirement, caused by the aggression of an irresponsible defender, prevents us from knowing whether he would have been capable of rolling back the limits of physical possibilities.

Among the contemporaries of the first period of Pelé's career, three of his compatriots attained the level of top international class. Didi, a field director of the first rank and impeccable technician, whose "folha seca" (the curved free kick) has become legendary; Garrincha, a winger famous for his dribbling and his unstoppable outflanking maneuvers; and Nilton Santos, the first attacking fullback of the postwar era. But the somewhat static play of the first, the limited field vision of the second, and the primarily defensive function of the third are factors that do not allow us to place these famous players on the same level as their incomparable teammate.

In this survey of the great players in international soccer around the year 1958, I could have cited names that have justly remained famous: Fritz Walter, whose talent and technical skill anticipated the evolution of German soccer; Stanley Matthews, the English magician of dribbling; Florian Albert, whose ease made people think that he might revive the great Hungarian era; Roger Piantoni of France, for whom nothing was difficult; the Czech Josef Masopust, who could do anything with a ball.

For different reasons and despite the immense prestige of Stanley Matthews, they never rose to the summits attained by those who came closest to Pelé.

What of today's "great ones"? Those who have bid adieu, like the English player Bobby Charlton; those who seem to be at the zenith of their career, like the Germans Franz Beckenbauer, Gerd Muller, and Günter Netzer, the Yugoslav Dragon Dzajic? Or those whose prestige has been on the rise, like the Dutchman Johan Cruyff, the Argentines Miguel Brindisi and Hector Yazalde, the Peruvian Teófilo Cubillas?

Charlton, survivor of the airplane crash at Munich that decimated the team of Manchester United, accomplished an admirable switch in 1966. From a steroetyped winger, he became a second center forward with amazing field vision, a veritable sparkplug. But during his direct confrontation with Pelé in Guadalajara, in an evenly matched encounter so far as team play was concerned, there was between the two men the difference that separates talent from genius.

Franz Beckenbauer, one of the key players of the West German team that conquered the world title in 1974, is an attacker who paradoxically occupies the position of last defender in front of the goalie, called "libero" or "sweeper." This enables him to avoid the tight guarding which his opponents exerted on him when he played at mid-field. It also enables him to start long counterattacks which are all the more spectacular since the massive retreat used systematically by many teams generally gives him a great deal of space in which to operate. The natural elegance of this tall, handsome athlete, his perfect technique and field vision, attract attention on his long runs. But because of the field he has to cover in his maneuvers and since he is evidently incapable of changing pace, Beckenbauer is not a real forward. His role remains limited to the initial phase of constructing attacks.

Gerd Muller is the antithesis of his teammate in Bayern Munich and the West German national team. Squat, with a long powerful upper body set on short legs and enormous thighs, a very quick starter possessing unusually alert reactions, Muller has an extraordinary goal instinct, as he demonstrated in the '70 Mundial, where he ended up as "goleador maximo," and in the West German league games.

It would be incorrect to say that he is merely an opportunist who instantaneously exploits an opponent's error. His constructive role is limited to being the pivot in the "give-and-go," but this is an extremely delicate role because he has to play it generally very close to the opponent's goal, surrounded by a pack of defenders who tackle mercilessly. All of which requires not only a solid physical resistance to withstand attacks but also a high precision in the return pass. But even if, when needed, he can start an offensive movement from a distance or participate in it, he has neither the range of action nor the mobility of a complete forward.

Günter Netzer, another important player in the German offensive line, possesses the attributes of what is called a "workhorse," that is to say, the means of covering a lot of ground. But although he also has the ability to eliminate opponents who are careless enough to attack him rashly, he rarely follows the offensive movement through to its conclusion. He lacks change of pace, like most mid-field players. And his failure in Spain, where he was a great disappointment in his first year with Real Madrid, can partly be explained by this deficiency.

A marvelous dribbler, less classical than Stanley Matthews, the Yugoslav Dzajic suffers from the defect of terminating his outflanking maneuvers by crosses that are too often inaccurate. He does not seem to believe in the cross that is pulled back to unbalance a defense. His shots are neither bullets nor on target. He cannot create for his partners the number of goal-scoring opportunities one would rightly expect from such a gifted winger. Hardly noticed in the 1974 World Cup, he has lost a good deal of his prestige.

The Argentine Hector Yazalde is at present by far the most productive center forward in Europe, since he has scored the impressive total of 41 goals in twenty-six league games for Sporting Lisbon. He thus confirms the hopes aroused in his native country three years ago where he was considered the best player of the new generation. For the time being it remains for him to prove himself in the great international contests which he did not have occasion to participate in prior to the 1974 World Cup.

Miguel Brindisi, his compatriot, is a mid-field player but of the offensive type, as attested by the great number of goals he has scored both for his club Huracan and for the Argentine national team. Unlike Beckenbauer and Netzer, he possesses the ability to accelerate which both Germans lack. It is, however, less certain whether this delicate and classy player is sufficiently resistant to fatigue and to tackles to rise much above the high level he has already attained.

Among the great modern forwards one could include Sandro
Mazzola, an apparently fragile player but endowed with extraordinary vitality. He seems to possess all the qualities one can
demand of a soccer player. Unfortunately, in the system of
counterattack imposed by Italian coaches, he can only occasion-
ally demonstrate the gifts that could have found complete
expression in a constructive and offensive context.

The same seems to apply to forwards as gifted as the Bulgarian Bonev, the Rumanian Dobrin, and the Paraguayan Arrua,
all of them victims of irrational systems of play that deprive them
of the support indispensable for full use of their great potential.

But let us go on to Johan Cruyff, who has made headlines as a
result of the manifest superiority of Ajax Amsterdam in the
European Champions' Cup for three years, of the colossal
amount paid for his transfer to Barcelona, and of the brilliant
career of the Dutch team which reached the Final of the 1974
Weltmeisterschaft.

Without doubt Cruyff is at present the most talked-about
forward in Europe. He scores goals, sets up goals for his teammates, plays the role of catalyst—if one is to judge by the resur-
rection of F. C. Barcelona. This triple achievement seems to
place him above Gerd Muller, Beckenbauer, and Netzer, the
great stars who could be used for purposes of comparison by those
who stick to established scales of value.

But it is important to take a closer look.

Cruyff a big goal scorer? Figures do not prove the point. Ajax
won the 1972–73 Dutch championship with a total of 102 goals
scored, but the most productive forward of the team was young
Rep, with 16 goals. His famous teammate does not figure among
the first four Dutch scorers nor among the forty best European
marksmen in national championship games. During his first year
at Barcelona and during the 1974 World Cup, Cruyff's showing
was no better. Until now no one has recorded the statistics of
Cruyff's goals for the simple reason that they add nothing to his
reputation. Far from it.

Cruyff sets up goals for his teammates? That is true. But when Barcelona committed the mistake of preferring Neeskens to Sotil, Cruyff, deprived of the services of the remarkable Peruvian playmaker, lost much of his prestige in Spanish stadiums.

Catalyst of a team's energies? Cruyff fulfilled that role in the Dutch national team. In Barcelona his arrival gave the Catalonian club an undeniable lift. For an objective appreciation it must be added that the previous season Barcelona had had the same players with the exception of Cruyff and the Peruvian Sotil, and that these players had obtained good results in the Spanish championship games, since they led the standings for a long time. But the Catalonian public criticized the Dutch coach Michels for his defensive attitude, which had provoked the eviction from the lineup of the two international Spanish forwards Marcial and Reixach. Being responsible for acquiring Cruyff—his pupil while he had been technical director of Ajax—Michels realized that in order to justify the high cost of the transfer (over $2 million), it was essential that he place him in favorable playing conditions, that is, surround him with players who would support him. Hence his return to an offensive attitude and the reinstatement of Marcial and Reixach in the forward line. The effects of this reconversion were revealed in Barcelona's brilliant victory in the 1973–74 Spanish championship games, where almost all the teams played very defensive ball.

This explains, in my opinion, the fortunate influence Cruyff's presence had on the production of his new team and the very flattering reputation it earned him. It would be risky to conclude that he possesses the means to transform a team in all circumstances. And Barcelona's total fiasco in the 1974–75 Spanish championship has completely confounded those who thought his bad showing in the 1974 Final in Munich was a mere accident.

But a soccer player who has attained the reputation of Cruyff must after all possess qualities that go beyond the ordinary. And indeed, Cruyff does have one that can be qualified as exceptional: a rapid start worthy of a top sprinter. For a striker that is an enormous asset, because it enables him to gain the decisive advantage of a few yards over the opponent or opponents assigned to guarding him. And since this lanky athlete, whose bearing resembles that of an alley cat, continues to move very rapidly once he is on his way, this physical quality opens up all the greater possibilities since his technical mastery, his vision, and his determination near the opponent's goal constitute so many trump cards.

But it must be emphasized that all this is based on the physical assets described above. Technically, Cruyff's repertory of feints is limited, as is clear when he receives the ball in a position where he cannot exploit his lightning start. His shots are neither bullets nor notable for their spin. In heading he has never assumed a dominating role. In the technical domain, despite his indisputable merit, he cannot stand comparison with Pelé, whose start is equally rapid, who moves as quickly with the ball, but who is much more powerful, possessing a repertory of feints, an arsenal of dribbles of infinite variety, and a personal effectiveness proven by figures that make any comparison impossible.

Yet it is in what constitutes the essence of soccer that an abyss separates Pelé from Cruyff. The Dutchman reads the game well, makes the pass that is called for when it is called for; but he is not the artist who makes the pass unexpected by all . . . except its receiver. He is not the creator who innovates and invents.

In summary one can say of Cruyff—as some have suggested—that he personifies today's soccer in the priority assigned to physical attributes. But that is not the kind of soccer, a popular and universal art, that crowds in all countries have come to see in Pelé.

Does this mean that the "King's" succession poses a problem that is unlikely to be resolved soon?

A priori it is difficult to admit that in a field where the number of participants increases constantly, quality should not spring from quantity. But in a team sport, the development of an individual depends on the conditions of his surroundings and the general milieu.

The case of Teófilo Cubillas is typical. This forward (who by a strange coincidence has been wearing the number 10, so difficult to live with since Pelé has turned it into a kind of symbol) is certainly the most worthy of the "succession." But he is Peruvian, and although he owes much to the Brazilian Didi—who turned the Peruvian team into the revelation of the 1970 World Cup—Cubillas has had to exile himself to Portugal in order to earn the money his qualities merit. A classy player, who possesses both power and suppleness, technical mastery and inspiration, Cubillas's nationality is likely to prevent him for a long time from conquering the World Cup, the crowning glory his immense talents deserve.

Not that it is enough to be Brazilian to succeed Pelé. Forwards apparently as gifted as Paulo Cesar, Rivelino, and Jairzinho have shown their limitations during the 1974 World Cup, which were less noticeable when, with Pelé at their side, they participated in the team play inspired by him. His departure has proved beyond doubt that technique, even when pushed to the limits of virtuosity, cannot replace personality and intelligence.

Tostao, who was called "the white Pelé," and before him Coutinho, the second prodigious child from the ranks of Santos, gave rise to the greatest hopes. The first, a magnificent, complete center forward, had to abandon soccer and the Brazilian team as a result of an accident that threatened his vision. The second did not have the will which is indispensable to overcoming difficulties in one's personal life.

These are some of the reasons why the "succession" remains open, and why the Brazilian government has repeatedly asked Pelé to play again for the national team in West Germany, in order to defend the World Cup conquered at Azteca Stadium.

9

A Soccer Genius

A few years ago anyone foolhardy enough to use the word "genius" during a conversation with intellectuals about soccer would automatically have been heaped with ridicule.

Like those who, in the name of intelligence, make a point of paying no attention to a phenomenon whose very universality and duration should incite them to reflection and analysis, the majority of coaches, officials, sports writers—the so-called sports intellectuals—display the same reaction today.

To be sure, when a player performs an unusual action in a soccer match, they are not insensitive to the beauty of the feat. And you will find it reflected in a newspaper headline or a sports column, since in sports material lyricism is regarded with favor—and "commercial" to boot.

But it is a far cry even from an article that qualifies such actions as "genius" to granting this superior form of intelligence the merit it rightly deserves. You will read all about the exceptional physical and technical qualities the feat required, for those are features the specialists are familiar with. But they will omit what is essential: the conception involved.

Why? For very simple reasons which I shall try to summarize here.

Since soccer has become an important branch of the entertainment industry and involves considerable financial and even political interests hidden behind the banner of national prestige, the factor of *producing*, of winning by any means, has replaced, under the term "realism," the pleasure of playing that is the fundamental condition of the art.

In the eyes of the industrialist-official in professional soccer, of the foreman-coach, and the sports writer won over to the religion of results, what do the more or less conscious aspirations on the part of players and spectators matter?

What counts is production, which means winning games or not losing, according to the current interpretation. This philosophy has given birth to the defensive reinforcement variously known as "béton" (French), "verrou" (Swiss), "catenaccio" (Italian), "cerrojo" (Spanish), "ferrolho" (Portuguese), or "sweeper system"—expressions of "realism" which sacrifice offensive creation and the risks it involves to the sacrosanct notion of security limited to counterattacks, chance speculations on an error by the opponent.

For the purposes of defending, of destroying, the role of intelligence is limited to carrying out orders of man-to-man guarding and to keeping numerical superiority on defense. Physical factors, on the other hand, are very important for annililating the efforts of opposing forwards, for intimidating them or eliminating them, by violent fouls if need be.

And since the forwards, in this same "realistic" conception, have but little opportunity for creation because they are outnumbered, the logic of the system makes them rely too on physical means.

Hence the ever greater care (and time) devoted to physical conditioning. In the eyes of the boss and his foreman-coach, physical fitness is a factor that can be measured by the stopwatch or the yard (running, jumping, etc.). And it fits in perfectly with a philosophy of life according to which work—unpleasant, hard, painful, boring work—is the indispensable condition of production.

Professional soccer players, following the pattern set by their Italian and British colleagues, have progressively accepted this way of looking at things in return for financial advantages that are frequently deceptive, since their career is brief and exposed to ever more numerous injuries. But by agreeing to sacrifice their intelligence to obeying orders, they have also killed the best in them: their faculty of creation.

And yet the best—and best remunerated—players of the "realistic" era are those who give the fans the opportunity to dream a little, those who have retained a little of that "romanticism" which it is fashionable to snicker at in the milieu of "serious" coaches, in short, those who are capable of sparking genuine inspiration. For one cannot indefinitely bring back the "suckers" who support the soccer industry by offering them an ersatz regional and national chauvinism in order to make them forget how little interest there is in the dreary gladiatorial combat soccer matches so often represent these days.

Meanwhile, manifestations of genius in the stadiums have become increasingly rare. The promises seen in highly gifted young players rarely come to fruition because, from early age on, their faculties are strangled by the teaching imposed on them by educator-coaches themselves formed in the school of "realism," and by the sickening spectacles television offers as the summits of the art of soccer.

How many Mozarts of soccer have been stifled in this way?

Pelé had the good fortune to have been born at a time when television was still in its infancy, when Brazilian soccer had no need of certified coaches, and when the joy of playing was of essential importance, even for professionals.

Well after he had been recognized as the greatest soccer player of all times, a visit to the Santos dressing room prior to a game showed me how faithful he had remained to the passion that ran in the veins of the "menino" of Bauru fighting over control of a rag ball with the brats in his street. Song and dance interspersed with slapstick, jokes, loud laughs, that was how the Santos players conceived of "psychological concentration" and the muscular warm-ups which so many European teams practice like a rite—the effect of which is certain to increase their nervous tension before entering the field and to deprive them of the free spirit and composure indispensable for maximum performance.

The joy of playing . . . Pelé has often spoken of it in significant terms. But it's enough to have seen him in action on the playing field in all kinds of circumstances, in a "tour" match played in Siberian temperature or in the rain in a World Cup game, to realize that the importance of the stake or worry about the outcome and its financial consequences always gives way for him to the pleasure of playing. "Alegria," joy. How many times have the reporters of Pelé's games used this word, which so aptly characterizes his behavior on the field and explains the ever new inventions expressed in astute, mischievous dribbles and feints.

Of course his starts, his breakaways, and his jumps, his sudden change of pace, his dribbling, his passes, make him "sweat," to use an expression dear to the theoreticians of the work-suffering-production philosophy. Soccer is a sport and as such it requires intense physical effort. But all soccer players will tell you that, when you play well, when you are having fun, you do not feel the effort. Jean-Marc Guillou, the best and also the most aware French soccer player of the past few years, told me recently: "There are games in which you go to the limit of your strength and you say: Already! when you hear the referee's whistle that ends the game."

There is no doubt that Pelé is physically superbly endowed. Although his height (5′9″) is relatively short for his weight of 165 lbs., on the field he gives an impression of balance, harmony, elegance, and ease which immediately strikes the observer. Anyone who has seen Pelé once will always recognize him again, even if the seat in the stadium is quite far from the turf, because it is impossible to confuse Pelé's appearance as a player with that of any other.

Doubtless, this impression is caused by the perfect synthesis of the physical qualities he possesses: power and suppleness, speed and resistance, spring and solid attachment to the ground. This blend of traits is expressed by muscular spurts near the opponent's goal: the tremendous head shots at Banks in Guadalajara and past Albertosi in Mexico City, the ultra-rapid slaloms, the incursions into defensive lines, or the bullet shots dispatched from any position. In the most difficult actions he always creates the same impression of balance, natural elegance, and harmony without ever showing off as Beckenbauer sometimes does.

It must be said that Pelé's technical mastery is total and always applied in the same way, no matter at what speed it has to be performed. All soccer players know those delicate situations in which, because the trajectory of the ball has been modified unexpectedly, or an opponent has suddenly intervened or a partner moved into position, an immediate adaptation is needed. Regardless of whether circumstances demand a sudden acceleration or an abrupt halt, the sequence of Pelé's motion always remains perfect, as if he had instinctively foreseen everything a fraction of a second ahead of everybody else.

While it is probable that there has never been a soccer player who possessed such an aggregate of athletic and technical qualities, it is certain that what distinguishes Pelé from his predecessors and contemporaries is his soccer genius. And not just occasional genius, for—this must be stressed—in any kind of match, even a mediocre one (and he does play mediocre ones), he always achieves one more or actions such as no one has ever accomplished before on a soccer field.

But what is genius?

Webster's dictionary defines it as: "Extraordinary power of invention or origination of any kind."

We often characterize genius in opposition to talent. Genius is inborn, intuitive, instinctive, creative; talent stems from reasoned intelligence and constant effort at improvement. Talent repeats flawlessly what has already been done; it does not create.

This classical distinction can help us to specify the notion of genius so far as soccer is concerned.

You can see many talented players in soccer stadiums, especially in top competition. They perceive the change of position or the move called for in a given situation because they possess the habit or the intelligence required for rationally constructed play and have the physical and technical means to carry out what they conceive. This intelligence is based on a logic that respects tactical principles born of experience.

Let us now turn to the case of Pelé's shot at goal from 65 yards in the game between Brazil and Czechoslovakia in Guadalajara.

Why did all the spectators have the same initial reaction: "He's crazy!"? Because they immediately drew the logical conclusion from a solid principle based on the experience of a century of soccer playing: you can't score a goal from such a distance, especially not in a game of that caliber. Pelé's action was contrary to logic, hence foolish, for common sense would have told him to go on moving the ball in order to set up a shot from a reasonable distance.

But when the same spectators saw the Czech goalie Viktor in vain pursuit of the ball heading for his net, they gave Pelé a standing ovation. They had just realized that this apparently foolish action was the one called for under the circumstances.

After the event, anyone could analyze the factors which justified this action: the advanced position of the Czech goalkeeper, the quickness, power, and accuracy of Pelé's shot. But no one except Pelé—who although involved in the game was in a far less favorable position than the spectators for a panoramic view of the field—could appreciate this. When one considers that the conception and execution of his shot required no more than fractions of a second, one can't help but be struck with admiration at this display of instinctive, intuitive intelligence which so brilliantly demonstrated its superiority over reasoned intelligence.

But the genius of this soccer player can be seen in far more complex accomplishments than the unexpected shot in Guadalajara, which was an individual action.

In team play a maneuver by the player in possession of the ball must simultaneously mislead the opponents and forewarn the partner to whom the pass is addressed. When it is a matter of the "last pass," the one immediately preceding the shot, this is particularly tricky.

In addition to all the qualities contained in the conception which inspired the now famous 65-yard shot, the last pass requires the ability to hint somehow to the pass receiver (who is out of the play and hence not considered dangerous by the opponent) that he is going to receive the pass and that he should get into better position to make use of it. Going into open position is an elementary principle of the game, and when the partner who has the ball is Pelé, one should always be on the alert. There are several ways of getting free, but only one ideal position to receive the ball on a full run exactly where Pelé is going to place it. Here mere logic is no longer enough. The pass receiver must also possess genius.

Coutinho showed genius at the Parc des Princes when, during the match against Racing in the Paris Tournament, he "sensed" that he must let Pelé's pass slip by him instead of returning it in the classical "give-and-go" maneuver. The entire Parisian defense was caught out of position by Coutinho's feint, which Pelé had "willed."

This power of suggesting to a partner what move to make is also used in "signaling" for the pass. During the game against Czechoslovakia in Guadalajara, by moving free on the wing, Pelé literally demanded the ball from Gerson at mid-field. Thanks to his exceptional physical and technical qualities, Pelé scored an unforgettable goal by controlling a ball received under very difficult conditions. But the genius displayed in this action lay in the sudden initiation of his move into the open and in the immediate response it evoked in Gerson's mind.

In soccer acts of genius are never pure individual, for partners of the player in possession of the ball must constitute at least elements of diversion. The "gol de placa" scored by Pelé in 1961 in Maracana Stadium, after a dribble begun in his own penalty area was possible only because his teammates as potential receivers of a pass he did not make, occupied the attention of the Fluminese players.

Even in average games one can see flashes of action that reveal a definite inspiration and prove that in every soccer player, as in any human being, there lies a genius of which he is unaware. But one cannot grant a player the epithet of "genius" if he does not repeatedly demonstrate the aptitude that "makes him capable of achieving an extraordinary power of invention or origination."

Pelé undeniably possesses this aptitude to a far higher degree than the other great soccer players and he demonstrates it far more frequently.

One day someone will certainly go beyond his achievements. The number of soccer players increases each year in the 141 nations controlled by FIFA, and sooner or later quantity is bound to give rise to quality.

But in order to discover Pelé's successor, the social environment which impedes the qualitative progress of soccer will have to undergo profound changes. For if, with rare exceptions, artists can no longer express themselves within the harsh confines of "modern soccer," is this not because such "realism" governs all social relations in the world today?

PART THREE

The Man and His Milieu

Having described Pelé's childhood and the principal stages of his athletic career—the exploits that brightened it and the mishaps that darkened it—and having tried to analyze the characteristics of the soccer player, it remains for us to try to understand the man.

This is a difficult task because Pelé has always jealously protected his private life.

We have seen with what lightning swiftness the kid from Bauru became a world-famous star at seventeen. From that time on, he has had to defend himself against the intruders who jostled each other at the exits of dressing rooms, at hotel entrances, in airport lobbies, and who telephoned him in the middle of the night. He has received thousands of marriage offers, as well as solicitations of all sorts ranging from mass requests for autographs, of course, to requests for money, and innumerable business propositions. Souvenir hunters have taken off with a considerable number of his famous shirts with the 10 on them and of course those shoes that enable him to score so many goals. There have been rumors that guerrilla fighters intended to kidnap him.

In 1959, during the South American Championship Games, the Brazilian team, hoping to find some peace and quiet, was quartered in a large suburb far from the center of Buenos Aires at the Hindu Club, reserved for members of the Argentine capital's aristocracy. Access to the buildings was under strict guard. But the precautions were useless. Pelé's room number was so quickly known that, constantly disturbed by intruders, he had to seek refuge for a siesta on the roof of the building where Bellini, his teammate, led me one afternoon so I could talk to him.

One can easily understand why, despite the gentleness and simplicity which astonish all those who come close to him, such a life of hounding and restless globe-trotting would exasperate him and lead to his decision to leave the Brazilian team. As he has repeated so often: "I want to devote myself to my family. My two children hardly know me, they see me come and go like a gust of wind. I want to be Edson Arantes do Nascimento again, a man just like everybody else, who will live like everybody else . . . "

It was also felt that the prospect of being once again in "concentraçao"—of having to go through the four months' intensive physical conditioning imposed upon players selected for the national team—was more than he was willing to put up with.

Materially, nothing seemed to stand in the way of the change Pelé had planned. The money he had earned in all the stadiums of the world, in movies, television, and radio, and from commercial advertisements was invested in apparently solid business enterprises.

But if you've got soccer "under your skin" and if, further, you are convinced that physically you've retained the means of continuing to play it as an artist, how could anyone have stayed in a retirement which everybody around them considered premature?

And so, less than a year after having left the Santos F.C. Pelé returned to active competition for three years, declaring that he would take part only in charity games, on June 15, 1975, in New York's Downing Stadium.

How are we to explain this startling volte-face by a man who had always kept his promises scrupulously?

Perhaps we shall be able to answer this better when we have gotten to know Pelé through the environment which spawned him and fashioned his personality: that of Brazilian soccer, Brazil itself, and the outside world.

10

Son of "Futebol"

In March 1966, the London *Observer* concluded a long study on Pelé with these words: "Pelé is the result of 50 years of soccer art in Brazil."

Indeed, Brazil has considered soccer a game and later an art ever since Charles Miller, a Brazilian of English extract, introduced the sport-of-the-round-ball in Sao Paulo. And a quip by a Brazilian enthusiast is also pertinent: "It wasn't the English who invented soccer. It was Pelé!"

Whereas European continental soccer never quite managed to liberate itself from its British origins and from the continued influence of Great Britain, Brazilian soccer has acquired a very strong personality as a result of its geographical distance from Europe, its particular climatic conditions, and its socioeconomic context.

Although since 1930 the Brazilian team has participated in the first and all subsequent World Cups, for a long while its international relations and those of its clubs had to remain limited to contacts with other South American countries—in particular, Uruguay and Argentina.

English soccer, played a great part of the time on rain-soaked fields, requires first and foremost great muscular strength, in order to kick a sodden ball, to move about on the often muddy pitch, and to bear the inevitable body contacts. Playing the game in a temperature frequently above 85 degrees and on dried-out ground necessitates adapting to different circumstances. The Brazilians did so quite naturally by transforming it into a sport in which skill took the place of strength, dodging the place of collisions; in which the muscular energy thus stored up was channeled into slowing down or speeding up the pace of the game.

Finally, the vastness of the country, the diversity of its population and cultures, its weak economic development, and the difficulty of communications prevented Brazilian soccer from adopting the standards of organization that the countries of the Old World had imported from England.

The originality of "futebol" is based on the three factors I have cited above.

So too is its strength. This has been proved not only by three conquests of the World Cup, the only competition of a truly universal nature (in 1958, 1962, and 1970), but also by getting third place in 1938, reaching the Final in 1950, and qualifying for all ten World Cups held since the first one back in 1930.

Because they did not come under the influence of players whose natural qualities and environment were entirely different from theirs, the Brazilians have preserved the unique personality of their soccer.

They certainly had things to learn, especially on the technical level, as can be seen from the results of the South American Championship in which Uruguay (the first world champions in history) and Argentina clearly have a superior record. But such lessons were not harmful. First because the students themselves drew the conclusions to be learned from their defeat in the living practice of the game; and second, because the "platensè" (technical short-passing) style had far more points in common with the Brazilian style than that of Great Britain or Europe.

The training methods used in England and rapidly adopted in Europe—methods based on intensive physical conditioning— found adherents in Brazil only much later, and then in a modified form. In 1958, the Brazilian team, during conditioning exercises prior to its match against France, drew condescending smiles from the "great" European coaches—particularly the Frenchmen. But this did not prevent that "ignorant" team from carrying off its hard-won world title a few weeks later.

For a long time the Brazilian players were safe from another danger: that of the "great national coaches," whose methods generally consist of copying what is being done elsewhere. Brazil has no school for coaches, no certificates issued by the mandarins of soccer science. Their coaches are former players who try to inculcate in the young the benefits of their experience without being either pedantic or authoritarian.

At the club level until recent years there has been the same absence of "structure," a key term of modern technocracy which European soccer has hastened to adopt. While it is true that the principal condition for becoming president of a club in Brazil is to have money or credit, the competition for this position is quite intense in a country where everybody loves "futebol" for its own sake. Opposed by numerous rivals, club presidents in Brazil do not have the kind of absolute authority they enjoy in Europe.

On the national level the same liberalism is evident, again imposed by circumstances. Each of the twenty-one states which make up Brazil has its own soccer federation, which organizes its own league competition for its own teams. All the federations are members of the "Confederaçao Brasileira de Deportos" (C.B.D.), but as its name indicates, this is an organization that rules over all sports, not only soccer. This inhibits it from exercising the same centralizing power as an exclusive federation, as is the case in all other countries.

The lack of organization which prevailed for a long time in Brazilian soccer both on the technical and general levels has in turn blessed it with an invaluable advantage: the liberty of expression and of creation without which one cannot speak of art.

As we have seen, Pelé is not the product of a soccer school; there was none in Bauru. Nor is he the product of the "realistic" conception of soccer imported from Europe. If Waldemar de Brito, his first coach at Bacquinho, had judged him in terms of physical strength, as do today's selectors of junior teams from six to eighteen in Europe, Pelé would never have been presented to the Santos coach. If Lula had required of his young hopefuls that they be built like an American football player, he would never have sent onto the field at Santo André the lean and lanky adolescent who drew such a look of pity from the referee.

Until 1970 physical appearance was never considered of primary importance by the great majority of Brazilian coaches. And even today when things have taken another turn, as we shall see later on, players such as Marco Antonio, Rivelino, Paulo Cesar, Dirceu, and others selected to play for the national team are far from corresponding to the canons proclaimed by the apostles of combat soccer.

In soccer, liberty of creation means liberty to play offensive ball. For a long time Brazilian players enjoyed that liberty, which enabled Leonidas, the "Black Pearl" of 1938, Tim, Romeu, and Domingo da Guia to amaze the French spectators during the 1938 World Cup, and Zizinho, Ademir, Jair, Danilo to outclass Spain and Sweden, Brazil's last two European opponents in the 1950 World Cup. In the Final against Uruguay, whose ferocious fighting spirit, defensive organization, and counterattacking tactics foreshadowed modern "realism," they succumbed, but they were the ones who gave the world an exalted vision of the art of soccer.

Pelé was ten years old at the time and he confesses that he wept when he learned that his idols had been defeated. Still, it was their example that inspired him and continues to inspire all Brazilian players.

Zézé Moreira, an early "realistic" coach, took the stand that the most "rational" lessons should be drawn from the tragedy of Maracana. And having succeeded in convincing the officials in power, he lined up a counterattacking team based on a stacked defense in the 1954 World Cup in Switzerland. But while people admired Julinho's outflanking maneuvers and his shots, Didi's clear field vision and his long pinpoint passes, they also noted the absence of the flamboyant team play illustrated four years before by Ademir, Jair, and Zizinho, the three musketeers of 1950. And they deplored the inevitable consequences of this style of play that runs counter to their temperament: incidents that marred the last 15 minutes of the game and continued in the dressing rooms after the deserved Brazilian defeat by Hungary and their elimination in the Quarter-finals.

With the failure of Zézé Moreira's conceptions at the very level he wanted to have them judged—in terms of actual results—Brazilian soccer returned to its natural sources, a decision which was to lead, no later than 1958, to the first of its three World Cup triumphs.

Does this mean that the player's liberty of expression is the panacea, the necessary and adequate condition for the flowering of the art of soccer? It is certainly one necessary condition, for in order to create, to carry into effect something that has never been done before, one has to take risks.

To be sure, a team sport by its very essence cannot do without rigorous principles of team play, which implies the adoption of an adequate tactical formation. But there are some playing systems that imprison the player and leave him no initiative, and others that enable him to express himself completely.

The 4–2–4 system is not a Brazilian invention. The great Hungarian team deserves credit for this tactical innovation, which was the result of a specific evolution, accomplished almost in a vacuum at a time when the cold war kept Hungarian soccer separated from the Western countries.

The reason the Brazilians adopted and popularized this tactical formation—the effectiveness of which they had experienced in their defeat at Bern in 1954—was because it corresponded perfectly with their concern to safeguard the liberty of expression of the player within a collective framework.

The balance between attack and defense contained in the 4–2–4 formation is only a starting point. In the application of rational play, which implies the aim of numerical superiority, this balance is abandoned by the participation of the two mid-field players on attack or defense according to what circumstances require. Moreover, since the backs are no longer tied down by man-to-man guarding and since the use of the zone defense requires the development of intelligence in positioning and in anticipation, the 4–2–4 system was quite naturally preparing the defenders to assume constructive and even offensive functions.

In 1958, Djalma Santos and Nilton Santos in particular were already very offensive fullbacks who did not hesitate to support their forwards. Those who observed the actions of the Brazilian fullbacks during the 1970 World Cup were struck by the mediocrity of Carlos Alberto and Everaldo in purely defensive tasks (their panic when the English pressed in attack toward the end of the game was quite evident), but also by their great constructive and offensive ability (the last goal of the Final scored by Carlos Alberto illustrates the case in point).

So Brazil carried off its most beautiful World Cup with ten attackers and a weak goalkeeper—a statement which constitutes the greatest homage to the artistic and offensive tradition of "futebol," and a brilliant demonstration of its practical effectiveness since the Italian team, its last victim, was (and remains) the most perfect incarnation of European defensive "realism."

How are we to explain then that, far from taking pride in the profound originality of their country's soccer, which had just been demonstrated in such a sparkling way, the directors and coaches, official representatives of Brazilian sports intelligentsia, hastened to look for imaginary reasons to explain this superiority? How are we to explain the fact that since the crowning ceremonies in Mexico City Brazilian clubs and the national team have adopted the identical defensive "realism" that had just been so thoroughly discredited?

Such an incredible ending to the Mexican epic triumph requires an explanation, for the millions who viewed the last World Cup—far more appalled by Brazil's closed and negative play than by its fourth place in the final standings—wondered how the successors of Pelé, Gerson, and Tostao could repudiate the style of play that was responsible for the glory of "futebol." It remains for us to examine the reasons for this sad metamorphosis.

A look at the official organ of the C.B.D. after the 1970 World

Cup is enlightening. First, the special edition, bearing the title: "Futebol do Brasil" IX Taça (cup) Jules Rimet.

While the cover of this de luxe brochure shows Pelé in action, the two opening pages are devoted to Mr. Havelange, then president of the C.B.D., with a summary of his biography and a declaration in which he reminds us that "he directed and organized the work of the Brazilian selection in view of the definitive conquest of the Jules Rimet Cup."

A historical summary of Brazil's participation in the World Cup since its inception and the presentation of the players crowned world champions in Mexico City follows. But the brochure very quickly returns to the C.B.D., its founding, its history, its administrative organization. Next comes an impressive chapter illustrated with superb photos and entitled: "The Biggest Stadiums in the World, which suggests clearly that the officials of the C.B.D. have supplied their soccer players with the material basis for their great achievements. To avoid any misunderstanding, the ensuing four pages are devoted to the titles and decorations of all the chief officials of the organization—one whole page to Mr. Havelange. The special edition of "Boletim" ends with a homage to Pelé and the complete record of the Brazilian team since 1914.

All of which is crystal clear: if Brazil is "tricampeao do mundo," it is due to a great organizer, namely, the president of the C.B.D. who, among other merits, has provided his country with the largest stadiums in the world, an impressive symbol of the country's prosperity and opulence.

For the Mini-Cup that the C.B.D. planned to organize in 1972, without hiding the fact that it was also the opening of Mr. Havelange's electoral campaign for the presidency of FIFA, this theme of "large stadiums" became the official leitmotif of the public relations blurb.

This delighted Sir Stanley Rous, then president of FIFA and intent on being re-elected. For, invited along with the international press to admire the great achievements of his rival, he noted that "the largest stadiums in the world" were most often three-fourths empty during the tournament, perhaps because of the abstention of several European soccer powers, among others England (accidentally, of course).

The reporters from the Old World who covered the competition also found out that the impressive façade of large stadiums hid an equally impressive scarcity of playing fields. At Bahia, for example, the teams of France, Africa, Argentina, and the CONCACAF (Caribbean Sea, North and Central America) experienced great difficulties in finding practice fields worthy of that name. Their complaints were in vain, for in Bahia, as in most of Brazil's large towns, small stadiums are rarer than anywhere else in the world, which is rather unexpected in a country in which "futebol" is the national passion.

For years travelers, tourists, and European reporters visiting Rio de Janeiro have been fascinated by the thousands of soccer players who can be seen every afternoon on the four miles of Copacabana Beach. This is indeed an amazing spectacle, but it would be wrong to consider it significant. For the "futebol de praia," also played all along the beaches of Botafogo, Ipanema, and Leblon, bears only a very superficial relationship to real soccer. On the soft sand the ball does not bounce and the player's supporting foot slips—conditions that require qualities and a technique quite different from the game played on grass or beaten earth. But it should be emphasized that to a naïve observer the picturesque spectacle of beach soccer masks the paucity of athletic facilities, in Rio de Janeiro particularly.

The amateur players are practically limited to a few fields surrounded by concrete gutters, their grounds covered with pebbles, their dimensions smaller than regulations require, on which pick-up teams play all day long and even into the night by the light of street lamps.

Obviously Mr. Havelange cannot be held responsible for this scarcity of fields, but it constitutes a reality which the existence of grandiose stadiums—built for prestige reasons—should not cover up.

If Brazil conquered three World Cups and does not owe them

to the material basis supplied for the mass of its players by the C.B.D., then to what does it owe them?

In Issues 11 and 12, dated December 1970, the official organ of the C.B.D. attempted to supply an answer to this question, under the title: "Chirol, Coutinho, and Parreira Show How We Won the World Cup." In thirty pages of a study filled with technical terms, comparative tables, calculated results, and tests of all sorts, the three physical trainers of the Brazilian selection during the Mexican campaign demonstrated that they had played an essential role in the conquest of the world title. One of them defined the mission they accomplished in these terms: "The era of empiricism in soccer belongs to the past. Henceforth we must use scientific methods to prepare our players."

A well-organized publicity campaign soon gave one of these "scientific methods" an extraordinary boost. The Cooper Test—a banal test which consists of covering the longest distance possible in 12 minutes—became the symbol of the utilization by soccer of the latest scientific discoveries. It was adopted by certified coaches everywhere, including those in charge of the French National Soccer Institute in Vichy. These neophytes discovered to their consternation that, while their pupils displayed abilities in foot races that were superior to those of the 1970 world champions, they also succeeded in occupying last place in the Third Division league standings.

Nevertheless, in Brazil the Cooper Test (imported from Houston, where it constituted one of the tests the astronauts had to undergo) became a sort of national institution. Every morning along the sidewalks of Copacabana Beach, sportsmen, influenced by the official propaganda, ran in sweatshirts while glancing anxiously at the signs indicating distance covered according to the Cooper Test.

Physical conditioning became one of the major themes of soccer columns when the Brazilian team was discussed. And the chief argument used to maintain the confidence of public opinion before the 10th World Cup Games was the time devoted to this preparation. Three and a half months of "concentraçao" . . . not one of Brazil's competitors had devoted half this time to group physical training.

It went without saying that this cult of physical preparation had the blessing of the C.B.D. officials, for it proved the lucidity and the seriousness with which they were directing "futebol."

Moreover, such an undertaking was expensive—a cost of some $2 million—and justified the eminent role of the president of the C.B.D., who had the necessary credit and relations to obtain this considerable investment in the name of national prestige.

While this myth of "scientific" preparation had been enjoying great success in Europe, it aroused increasing skepticism among Brazilian players and in well-informed circles. First of all, because the way national competitions are organized in Brazil practically rules out any kind of practice for professional clubs.

For financial reasons that become even more urgent when a World Cup draws near (the clubs are deprived of their best players selected for the Brazilian team over a period of four months), the C.B.D. is forced to increase the number of competitions in order to boost the clubs' finances and to compensate them for the loss of attraction.

Contrary to a widely held belief in Europe, professional clubs in Brazil lead a very precarious existence. And this situation dates far back.

In 1969 the important daily *O Estado de Sao Paulo* conducted an inquiry entitled: "They Want to Live," which revealed that ten of the clubs in the Paulista League were "in their death throes." Along with figures showing the financial deficits of Botafogo Riberao Preto, Comercial, and America, this paper published statements by players who had not been paid for more than four months and reports of insolvency by club presidents. The disparity between the great Paulista clubs and the numerous provincial teams was expressed in telling figures. The receipts of the "greats"—Corintians, Santos, Palmeiras, Sao Paulo F.C.—were 100 to 200 times superior to those of provincial clubs!

In Rio the disproportion is the same. Recently *Placar*, a specialized magazine, devoted an alarmed article to the situation of the small clubs in the professional Carioca League under the headline: "Receipts: 2,532 cruzeiros. Paying spectators: 422." It concerned a game between Madureira and Portuguesa; beneath photos of a small, empty, and decrepit stadium, the caption read: "This is not a little match in a hamlet lost somewhere in the interior of Brazil, but a match of the Carioca League."

And the article concluded:

"In the country that won the soccer world championship three times, this is a depressing spectacle, a demonstration of the deficient structures of professional soccer."

It must be added that the facts cited by *Placar* are not exceptional and that in states less favored than the state of Guanabara (to which Rio belongs), the situation of the professional clubs is far more serious. In a league game of the Ceara Championship involving Quixada and Tiradentes on May 5, 1973, the receipts amounted to 676 cruzeiros, some $100!

Despite their impressive receipts the great clubs are experiencing inextricable financial difficulties. Botafogo, the great Carioca club, with five players "requisitioned" by the national team, was on the brink of bankruptcy on April 19, 1974, with a deficit of more than $1 million. Mr. Rivaldivia Meyer, its president, declared in a report released to the press:

"We have reached a dead end. Brazilian soccer is crying for help. We have put up our stadium, our club house, and our offices for auction. We are ready to sell them to the highest bidder in order to pay our debts. . . ."

This is a far, far cry from the idyllic picture of Brazilian soccer wallowing in opulence which the bulletins of the C.B.D. depict.

On the basis of these data it is easy to imagine the living conditions of the great majority of the 7,150 professionals (the number cited in the C.B.D. "Boletim"). A study devoted to this subject, again by the magazine *Placar*, showed that, while some twenty stars obtained monthly revenues above $2,000, the great majority of Brazilian "pros" received absurdly low salaries (around $100), when they happened to be paid.

In order to improve the situation of the "recuperable" clubs

alone, the C.B.D. three years ago organized a national championship (Campeonato Brasileiro) which in 1973 took on extravagant
proportions with the participation of forty clubs dispersed all
over Brazil.

The "biggest soccer championship in the entire world"—so
the press presented this monstrosity, which began in August 1973
and finished in February 1974 after 656 games divided into a preliminary and a final round.

The rules of this inflationary championship contained a provi-
sion that is shocking on the sporting level: the big clubs were
authorized to play all their games in the stadiums of the "little
ones," since their prestige would be a guarantee of good receipts,
of which they received the greater share. They thus accepted to
play without return match on the opponent's field for financial
advantages. By contrast, the meetings among "big" teams respected the home-and-home system.

The consequences of this rule, established exclusively for financial reasons, turned out as one might have expected. During
the preliminary round, the standings presented a flattering and
completely false impression of the strength of certain small clubs
that had the advantage of playing very frequently at home. The
table of receipts which the press often published next to the
standings revealed a different reality: the hierarchical standing
of receipt producers, at the head of which stood Santos, due to
Pelé's presence on the team. The final victory of Palmeiras, a
"big" club, preserved the appearance of fair play.

But it was an appearance only, for Palmeiras, in order to win
the national title, had to play forty games in addition to twenty-
two matches in the Sao Paulo Championship and others during
tours. This represents an average of two games per week and
unending flights necessitated by the dimensions of a country as
vast as a continent.

"Where and when could the Brazilian players have engaged
in the joys of the Cooper Test? In airport lobbies?" Hans Henningsen asked ironically on Rio's Radio Continental.

Anyway, what we do know is that at the end of this marathon

the players selected for the Brazilian team showed up early in March in a state of fatigue close to exhaustion at the Retiro de os Padres, the "concentraçao" camp, and that they demanded time to rest up before putting themselves in the hands of the trainers. The result of the first game on their training program was significant: a score of 1–1 against the weak Mexican team eliminated from the World Cup by Haiti and thrashed by Trinidad.

Furthermore, the proliferation of games for financial reasons had a very grave effect on the playing style itself.

From a series of articles published in *Miroir du Football* under the title "Whither Brazil?" by the two Brazilian correspondents Solange Bibas and Hans Henningsen, I excerpt these lines dated September 1973:

At present the most frequently used word in Brazilian soccer is "retranca." It needs no translation, being so close to English "retrenchment." In technical language it is the equivalent of "béton," "catenaccio," or "cerrojo." Traditionally the symbol of offensive play, Brazilian soccer is now becoming the symbol of defensive play. Scoreless ties are booming. In the last 46 games of the Paulista League a total of 72 goals have been scored, i.e. an average of 1.5 per match. During one playing date four games have resulted in 0–0 scores or 360 minutes of play for nothing! . . . A "little" team in the League, Juventus, has played 13 games without conceding a goal. . . . A corollary of "la retranca" is violence, I would even say the systematic assassination of the forwards. "Artilheros" such as Pelé, Cesar, Vaguinho, Edu are subject to constant aggressions. . . . Pelé has stated: "Attacking ball is about to die because the forwards who penetrate into the penalty area are systematically cut down by violence."

For his part Hans Henningsen underlined the influence that the financial preoccupations of the clubs had had on the deterioration of Brazilian soccer three years after its brilliant offensive demonstration in the Azteca Stadium:

Making money has become imperative, for the clubs now have considerable expenses to meet. They must, of course, pay the salaries of their players, but also the salaries or bills of a superabundant per-

sonnel. Until recently only coaches and players were remunerated. Today we must add to these the trainers, the specialists of the Cooper
Test, physicians, dieticians, masseurs, orthopedists, dentists, super-
visors, observers, etc. . . . Money has to come in regularly to make all
those people live. And the surest way is not to lose on the field. Which
explains the 0–0 scores. . . .

Hans Henningsen also showed the influence of "soccer pools"
on this evolution of "futebol":

"The bettor does not go to the stadium to see the game but in
the hope that the result will agree with what he has written on
his betting card. Thus it matters little whether the match totally
lacks interest as a sport, whether the laws of the game are vio-
lated, whether violence reigns. . . . Only the result counts."

And when Tostao, after having undergone a second eye oper-
ation, decided to abandon soccer, he got a few things off his
chest:

"The first words a defender says to me when I enter his penalty area are always the same: 'If you get close to me, I'll break
your leg.' One of them recently found a new one. He said to me:
'Be sure to protect your good eye. You only have one left!' "

We have come to the provisional end of the process started by
the "structuring" of Brazilian soccer associated with Mr. Havelange before he announced his candidature as director of world
soccer.

By imposing on "futebol" an organization based on the same
principles and institutions as in the European countries, he has
killed his personality, rendering it a carbon copy of that incarnation of anti-soccer crushed by Brazil in Mexico City.

No doubt he did not intend to do this, and became aware of
his error as the 10th World Cup drew near, since after having
declared: "If Pelé wants to play in Germany, the doors of the
team are open, but I shall not solicit him," he made two official
attempts to have him change his mind and even considered using
the means of pressure the rules placed at his disposal.

Without Pelé—and without Tostao and Gerson, the two other
children of "futebol"—the Brazilian team turned out to be just

another team. For the first time in its history the abundance of first-rate defenders underlined the weakness of its attackers.

But is not this evolution of "futebol" a faithful reflection of the evolution of Brazilian society? Can today's Brazil give birth to a great ball artist and place him in conditions favorable to his full development?

11

God Is Black

In no other country does soccer occupy the place in everyday life it has in Brazil, a fact that has struck all European observers, including those who normally assign no importance to sports matters.

In a book entitled *Brazil*, published in 1958, Pierre Jouffroy wrote:

While it is true that people swim, ride horses, drive (in Maseratis or on bicycles), box, jump, race on foot in Brazil, all this is really unimportant. There is only one thing that matters: "futebol" which is, along with the lottery, the ruling and destructive passion of the people. A stadium with a capacity of 150,000 to 200,000 spectators in Rio (the largest in the world) is hardly big enough for the noisy fans on Sundays. Drums and firecrackers rhythmically accompany the rushes of the center-forwards. A goal scored always causes the death of one or two cariocas in the stands. . . . For fifteen or twenty years the Brazilians have been the best players in the world, but an incomprehensible fatality had always made them fail in the World Cup. They had to wait until 1958 for the Brazilian team to turn this dream into reality. Thereupon the President of the Republic interrupted his consultations, Rio improvised its Carnival for a day, and the churches offered thanksgiving services. Emotionally such a victory represents a national advancement, the liquidation of the last remaining colonial complex.

In 1966 Jean-Jacques Faust, after five years spent in Brazil as director of the Rio office of the Agence France-Presse, published a sociopolitical work entitled *Brazil, An America for Tomorrow*. The jacket is illustrated by a photo of Pelé being carried in triumph by fans. Several pages are devoted to the "black god." An interesting excerpt follows:

> The god of soccer appeared to me one evening in a bundle of light rays on the turf of Maracana in the guise of a resplendent black athlete whose name is Edson Arantes do Nascimento but whom his people, all his people, adore under the name of Pelé. You may not understand the rules of the game, but you cannot help but admire Pelé's grace. Ferocious with his opponents, whom he confuses by the quickness of his powerful and unpredictable movements, tender with the ball, which he handles as one would caress a woman. . . . The god of soccer, Pelé is naturally a national hero.

The author continues with a description of the three goals scored that evening by Pelé and the reactions of the crowd:

> Maracana Stadium exploded. Firecrackers from everywhere. Some people were weeping, others were laughing, still others dancing. . . . My Brazilian neighbor, who I did not know and who, until then, had seemed relatively calm, jumped up, took me in his arms, slapped me on the back until it hurt and, without letting go of me, broke into a samba step. "Isn't it beautiful?" he kept repeating in a voice hoarse with joy. If I had contradicted him, he would probably have killed me. The next day the newspapers reported that three spectators had had heart attacks. They had nearly died from too much pleasure.
>
> The god of soccer, Pelé is naturally a national hero. Every Brazilian knows his biography by heart. A Brazilian who is not a "torcedor" is like a Frenchman who does not eat bread. Soccer is the subject of two out of three conversations.

These extracts from Pierre Jouffroy and Jean-Jacques Faust are of special interest because they are not the work of specialized sports writers and hence cannot be suspected of overrating the importance of what they saw.

You will have noticed that both assign to "futebol" a political importance, the first stressing what Brazil's victory in the 1958 World Cup represents ("a national advancement, the liquidation of the last remaining colonial complex"), the second emphasizing Pelé's tremendous popularity and broaching the racial question in these terms: "The fact that the only unquestionable Brazilian hero is a Black constitutes a social phenomenon of the greatest importance."

The conclusions the two French writers have in common, as we shall see, is the attempt to analyze the relationship between "futebol" and Brazilian society.

It is entirely correct, first, that the passion of Brazilians for "futebol" is shared by all classes of society. The same does not hold true in Europe. In England, for example, soccer has remained the sport of the working class, even though members of the middle classes and even of the nobility take an interest in the dividends they can earn by financial investments in the corporations that the big clubs of the professional league have formed. In every country in the world the spectacle of soccer attracts people belonging to all social strata, even though the great majority of participants and spectators come from the lower classes. All the same, even in England, the cradle of soccer, there are noble sports such as tennis, track, and horse racing, while soccer is banished from the program in schools reserved for the gentlemen of tomorrow.

In Brazil "futebol" is *the* sport, and on Copacabana Beach as on the pebbly fields along Flamengo Bay, youngsters and adults come down from the "fabelas" and the inhabitants of the white buildings at Copacabana face each other in mixed teams in daily matches.

This omnipresence of "futebol"—the importance the subject occupies not only in conversation but in the press, on radio and television, in the cinema, in literature, and in politics—can be traced to deep-seated national feelings. Although Brazil ceased being a Portuguese colony in 1822, because of its economic dependence it suffered for a long time from an inferiority complex from which the sports victory has helped to liberate it.

This is why, in the eyes of an observer unconnected with sports, Pelé is "the only unquestionable Brazilian hero." Quite simply he embodies the aspirations for dignity of all Brazilians; better than the Heads of State who have succeeded each other since 1958 in governing the country, better than the greatest names in literature, painting, architecture, and cinema. None of these Heads of State, none of these big "names" has taken the slightest offense ever since, in 1962, President Janio Quadros officially proclaimed Pelé a "national treasure"; and all his successors, despite their profoundly differing political views, have showered him with official honors.

It is nonetheless true that for a young Black from the "favelas" and for an industrial tycoon from Sao Paulo "futebol" does not have the same profound meaning.

For the former, Pelé is himself, because he has the same skin color, because he was a poor boy who played barefooted with rag balls for lack of money to buy himself shoes and a real ball.

Officially racism has no place in Brazil, whose 100 million inhabitants have sprung from the greatest known mixture of races; in fact, most of them would be unable to state what kind of blood they have in their veins. Europeans of various nationalities, Africans, Asians, indigenous Indians have all made unequal but important contributions to the formation of the population.

Nonetheless, all foreign observers agree in adding a "but" . . .

Jean-Jacques Faust says:

"While it is true that in Brazil one encounters no trace of organized segregation, formally prohibited by law, it is no less true that there exists a consciousness or, if you prefer, a perception of color."

And after citing Pelé's remarks on the Black problem: "I am happy to be both Black and a good soccer player, for I can thus make my contribution to racial democracy in my country," he adds:

"Pelé's observations fall in line with this opinion by Jacques Lambert, professor at the Faculty of Law at Lyons, whose expertise on Brazilian problems is universally recognized: 'Color is certainly a blemish in Brazil, but it is not an irreparable blemish: being black is not a defect impossible to overcome; however dark one's skin may be, one is no longer a negro when one is well brought up, educated, or wealthy.' "

In his book *The Twenty Latin Americas*, Marcel Niedergang, another specialist in Latin American problems, expresses an almost identical point of view in these terms:

In the final analysis, the boundary [between Whites and Blacks] is more economic than purely racial. If one studies this question on graphs, one finds that the different levels of living standards correspond generally to precise categories of skin color. In Brazil the very wealthy are generally white and the very poor most frequently black. The real solution of the racial problem is economic in nature, and not psychological. It is less a question of fighting against prejudices, which are scarcely noticeable, than of improving the standard of living of the masses.

A similar view is contained in a reply by Pelé to a reporter on the magazine *Africasia* who asked him whether the Black problem existed in Brazil:

"I don't believe so. In my country the black race is not equal to the white race, but it is nearly so."

This "nearly" accurately describes the existence of a problem that has been treated in its relationship with soccer by the Brazilian journalist Mario Filho, whose name is inscribed on the façade of Maracana Stadium. It helps us to understand what "futebol" represents for the Brazilian Blacks, insofar as they are members of the economically most disadvantaged social group in the country.

For young Edson Arantes do Nascimento, the son of an underpaid professional player who later became totally unemployed, it represented first, a game, that is to say: a means of expression. Then the hope of overcoming poverty, of rising toward dignity. Even though he became "King Pelé," he has been so marked by that period of his life that he still speaks of it constantly.

Sometimes he does so to justify his tendency to save money, as when he stated: "I know that when I am no longer Pelé, I'll be a Negro. . . ."

More frequently it is because his sensitivity, which easily moves him to tears, leads him to identify with the "meninos" who live as he did and who dream as he did. It was to them that he spontaneously dedicated his 1,000th goal, immediately after scoring it on the field, still trembling with emotion, as his interviewers emphasized.

Besides the sad and painful memories of his early youth, Pelé finds in the children the pure joy and exalting hopes of the "futebol" of the "peladas"—those improvised matches in which one lines up according to one's preferences without worrying about the number of players, often more than fifteen to a team.

In Sao Paulo there is a championship with the picturesque name of "Dente de Leite" (milk tooth), reserved for children ten years of age. Whenever he finds the time, Pelé is an attentive spectator. A few years ago he was singing the praises of a "negrinho" by the name of Carlos Roberto Bento, already honored by his partners and opponents with the distinction of a nickname (Bizzi) which is only given to prospective stars. Pelé was no doubt particularly happy to learn that his discovery, voted most valuable player of the competition, had hastened to offer his father a part of his first "bonus:" one of the three pairs of shoes he received from the organizers.

What Pelé has retained from his childhood is the love of "futebol" for its own sake. Whatever may be at stake in the game he is playing, he is having a good time on the field. That is where he gives vent to his *joie de vivre*, where he expresses himself completely. For this reason he is an artist first and only secondarily a professional player. For the most famous and highest paid player of all times soccer is never real work, a chore that has to be done to come out on top or to justify his fee.

I have sometimes seen him looking melancholy in a hotel lobby an hour before game time. But as soon as he entered the dressing room, the laughter started. He was in his element.

During the winter of 1973, at Liège, in a cold rain, Santos

was finishing an exhausting tour begun under the burning sun of the Middle East. Two days before, without transition, the Pelé Football Club had played in Nuremberg on a frozen field.

Against the spirited and tough Standard team, familiar with the rigors of European winters, the Santos players were giving signs of weakening on the muddy turf of Sclessin Stadium. Pelé, after having performed some of the exploits only he can do, realized that it was time to devote himself to humble tasks which some of his partners were unable to take on. Coated with mud, he began to cover mid-field, defending like a fullback, fighting with all his strength so that his team would retain the advantage of the goal scored by Edu on a breakaway.

In the dressing room, where I expected to find a man in bad humor, he was smiling and happy to have managed to carry out a task to which he had devoted himself like the most loyal of team players.

It is however probable that he would not like to go through this kind of experience too frequently. To him soccer means scoring goals or creating scoring opportunities for his partners.

This thirst for goals and the happiness he experiences when he succeeds in scoring has been defined by Pelé in vivid terms:

"When the ball is about to get to me while I am in scoring position, I watch for it as if it were a drop of water that is going to fall on my dried-out tongue. When I take it with my foot or my head, when I see it hitting the back of the net behind the goalkeeper, when I hear the shouts of the crowd, I feel a total exaltation that electrifies my body and my mind. . . . For me it is the most complete of all joys. . . ."

But can one be the greatest soccer player, and especially the greatest goal scorer, without possessing deep down a certain form of aggressiveness?

Brazilian psychologists have studied Pelé's case and concluded in the affirmative.

The shot at goal, as Pelé has also emphasized, is "like an explosion" that liberates pent-up energy for the success of the decisive action.

Only someone who has never experienced this sensation

would be amazed that the total liberation of this suppressed force will give rise to gestures of delirious joy—such as Pelé's jumping high and striking the air with his fist, his trademark since the '70 Mundial.

But this basic and undeniable aggressiveness—which all human beings possess to some degree, since it is the heritage of a social milieu in which the struggle for life remains a reality—is not used by Pelé to harm the physical health of his opponents.

In the jungle that soccer has become in the era of "realism," he has the physical means to get himself respected, if need be. And being constantly at close quarters with defenders who use intimidation and violence, it has happened that he has reacted with a violence unexpected for one of his natural gentleness. The German Giessman and the Argentine Messiano were two of his notorious victims in 1965, and Pelé expressed none of the hypocritical regrets that are customary in such cases.

But he realized very soon that on the field the struggle was useless. A forward, because his sole objective is the ball and because he often has his back to the opponent, is too vulnerable a target for a fullback intent on attacking him. Jetchev and Morais cynically exploited this advantage to put him out of action during the 1966 World Cup.

That painful experience added to many others explains the period of discouragement he went through after his return from England and his decision never to play again in the World Cup.

Furthermore, all those close to Pelé know that he has always been haunted by the fear of suffering his father's fate, rendered unemployable by a kick on the knee from an opponent during a match.

An article devoted to this subject by the *Correio de Manha* in 1969 concluded: "Pelé has three phobias: poverty, professional insecurity, and the fatality that put an end to his father's career."

Facts prove that he has overcome these fears, which still bothered him frequently prior to the departure of the Brazilian team for Mexico in 1970. Justified fears when one recalls the aggressions by the Uruguayans on him during the Semi-final and by the Italians, particularly Bertini, in the final game. Fortunately the Mexicans—who were very favorably disposed toward the Brazilians because of their fondness for the artistic conception of soccer embodied by Pelé and his partners, and were evidently hostile toward the English whose manager had insulted the host country—somewhat limited both the amount and the seriousness of the brutal acts by inducing the European referees to be less tolerant with "realists."

However, there can be no doubt that the deterioration of soccer has played a large part in Pelé's decision not to participate any more in a competition in which the will to win justifies the use of any means and, primarily, violence. The remarks quoted above, taken along with the equally unmistakable remarks by Tostao, are significant.

He did not pronounce them out of spite, for according to all observers of the Paulista Championship and the 1974 National Championship, in both competitions he showed brilliant form, characterized by the title "artilhero."

But the ever-increasing roughness of the game made him lose part of his joy in playing, and while he managed to preserve it in his performances for Santos, he feared that things would be different with the Brazilian team—especially during the four months of "concentraçao" prior to departure for West Germany.

It is also true that other factors influenced his stand: family considerations, of course, and considerations pertaining to his numerous outside activities.

His first incursion into the business world did not turn out well. The small factory of sanitary articles, "Sanitaria Santista," in which he had invested his first savings in association with his teammate and brother-in-law Zito, had been badly run by their trusted manager. Against the advice of his friends Pelé categorically refused to resort to legal action, despite the financial losses he had suffered.

A few years later Pelé had a financial interest in a modern factory producing synthetic fibers under the trade name of "Fiolax." He had an executive office in the building of one of the biggest Brazilian banks, the Banco de Campinas. He starred in a television serial in the role of a detective. In a feature film *A*

Marcha (The March), he played the leading role as a former slave fighting against the landowners. He took part in TV variety programs as singer and accompanied himself on the guitar in his own compositions.

Brands of clothing, shoes, watches, bicycles, soccer balls, chocolate bore his name and brought him important royalties.

The street in Tres Coraçaoes containing the house he was born in and the new 80,000-seat Maceio Stadium (the Stadium of King Pelé) were named after him.

The subject of biographies, novels, and poems, with his picture on stamps issued by the Brazilian postal service, Pelé has attained a level of celebrity unequaled by any other Brazilian.

But while he has been officially received by all the Presidents who have succeeded each other at the helm of his country's government, he always managed to keep his distance from the politicians in power.

People were surprised when, in 1969, he gently but firmly refused an invitation to lunch with the powerful governor Negrao de Lima. His decision to bid adieu to the Brazilian team on July 18, 1971, was made against the advice of Joao Havelange, then president of the C.B.D., whose resentment was expressed first by the absence of any official ceremony and then by indifferent statements ("He may return if he wants to, but I shall not solicit him").

When, early in 1974, Mr. Havelange was forced by pressure of public opinion to solicit him and suffered a rebuff, he made a veiled allusion before the press to an article in the rules of the C.B.D. obliging any Brazilian player to report when called upon to play on the national team or risk punitive action. Pelé immediately replied: "If this threat is carried out, I shall give up soccer at once, and the C.B.D. can take care of the debts of the Santos Football Club."

He likewise declined the "suggestions" of the President of Brazil, General Garrastazu Medici, who added his voice to that of Mr. Havelange.

Joao Saldanha had been equally courageous in 1970, when

the Head of State, eager to maintain his popularity in Belo Horizonte, publicly advocated the selection of Dario (the striker of Atletico, one of the big clubs of the capital of Minas Gerais). Saldanha had to leave his position as national coach. He stated on television: "The Head of State directs the State. The director of the selection directs the selection and in his opinion Dario has no place in it. . . ."

Those outside Brazil who reproach Pelé for not having taken a position in the political field and for having been "co-opted" by the government are ignorant of these facts and their full implications in Brazil today.

This holds true for certain journalists, like the one from the magazine *Africasia* published in Paris who asked him questions such as:

"What do you think of the dictatorship in your country?"

Or this one:

"How many dollars do you own?"

And finally:

"You are one of the biggest millionaires, particularly among the Blacks, in Brazil. Don't you feel bad to have so much money when the majority of the Blacks live on the margin of society, when 60 percent of the population—90 percent of them—live in inhuman conditions?"

A questionnaire of this sort reveals strong tendencies toward the very same "sensational journalism" that the magazine is supposed to be attacking.

The frivolity and ignorance of the inquiry were confirmed by another naïve question:

"Did you ever happen to live in a favela?"

To which Pelé replied: "You will find poor people living in other places as well as the favelas," without considering it useful to let him know that, contrary to the statements of many journalists, he had indeed known poverty and hunger.

But while it is a confession of ignorance to ask Pelé, living in Brazil, what he thinks of the "dictatorship in his country," one has of course the right to judge his attitude on the economic and political situation there without trying to elicit statements that might have grave consequences.

And when questioned on this subject, Pelé also has the right to reply: "I am not a politician, I am a soccer player . . ."

Nevertheless, Pelé is perfectly conscious of the true situation of the great majority of the Brazilian population, which has no share in the substantial profits of the "economic miracle" illustrated by official indices of growth. Indeed, he is so conscious of it that no one ever had to solicit from him numerous declarations "not to forget the fate of poor children." It is also known in Brazil that he does not limit himself to high-sounding phrases and that he does not boast of his generosity.

Those who are revolted by injustice and torture would like to see Pelé "commit himself" in the struggle, to place his prestigious name at the service of a great cause. They readily compare him with Muhammad Ali, who has become the advocate of the emancipation of the American Black.

But it is impossible to compare the conditions in which the two most famous Black athletes of our times live. In the United States, Muhammad Ali can carry out his political activities in broad daylight. To a great extent the law gives him this right, even though his refusal to do his military service cost him a lengthy suspension in his athletic career and considerable financial loss. In today's Brazil, a "commitment" of that sort would result in quite a different fate for Pelé.

The Black problem is very different in the U.S.A. and in Brazil. The admixture of the majority of the Brazilian population rules out racism in the acute form in which it exists in North America.

Pelé has been photographed embraced (his body and face covered with soap) by Robert Kennedy, candidate for the presidency of the United States, in the dressing room at Maracana.

"Kings, dictators, Presidents of Republics, governors have always treated me with the greatest respect. I have behaved in the same way toward them, the same way I behave with completely unknown spectators who come toward me in a stadium," he replied to a reporter on the magazine *Veja* who had asked whether he was insensitive to the problem of racism.

But even though he has married Rosemary Cholbi, a white woman employed in a bank and from a modest family, even though his daughter Christina and his son Edson need not fear contempt from some of their compatriots, he is perfectly conscious of the fact that his fame and fortune have enabled him to escape the precarious condition in which the majority of Brazilian Blacks live.

To go further, to question the sociopolitical foundations of the current Brazilian régime, would require a higher degree of political consciousness.

Those Brazilians who have committed themselves to a fight that requires far more courage have never held it against him that he has not joined them, even though they regret it.

But it would be wrong to think that Pelé, who since the age of seventeen has always amazed his interlocutors by his maturity of mind, is blind to the problems of his time.

Speaking about the revolt of young people to a reporter of the *Folha de Sao Paulo*, he made these revealing statements:

"The young people of today want to build, but not along beaten paths. They are looking for new horizons. . . . Life did not permit me to be like these young people because since the age of sixteen my time has been taken up with travels, training, matches, and 'concentraçaos.' I did not have the time to reflect as much as others during that period of my life. . . .

"When we are young, we always ask ourselves many questions, but nobody has the time to answer them. We are always rushed in life, we run all the time. We, I, you, we ought to do something to change the world. Technique, science, everything evolves except the mind of a man who is late. . . . The fact that the young are protesting proves that they don't want to be late."

By the unaffected simplicity of his behavior, by the enormous reverberations of his athletic exploits, by the noble attitude he has displayed on the field in the most popular sport in the world, it could be said that Pelé has, in the final analysis, served the cause of the Blacks and the humble more effectively than Muhammad Ali in certain ostentatiously violent gestures and his participation in the great mystique of the boxing business.

In any case, it is undeniable that Pelé's name everywhere evokes the humane and artistic image that the Brazilian people have been able to give to a sport invented by English workers at the end of the nineteenth century.

12

Unanimously Acclaimed

Aside from the great competitions and international matches he has played with the Brazilian team in America, Europe, and Africa, Pelé since 1958 has taken part in innumerable Santos tours in regions as far removed from the European–South American axis as Thailand, Indonesia, Japan, Australia, Canada, Africa, Saudi Arabia and Dubai.

In the *Miroir du Football* Solange Bibas, who followed Santos on one of these tours, gives us an idea of what it involved:

"120 hours of flying time, 14 games in one month, changing from a 103° temperature to 13° in less than 24 hours with stops in New York, Los Angeles, Honolulu, the Fiji Islands, Sydney, Ryad, Qatar, Bahrain, Khartoum, Dubai, Nuremberg, Liège, Coventry, London, Rio, Sao Paulo. . . ."

Of these fourteen games (played at 48-hour intervals at places sometimes thousands of miles apart) Santos lost only one; it could be said that the players earned their money.

Pelé, without whom Santos would not have gotten half their game contracts, was the only survivor of the team that began these trips over fifteen years ago. Considering that he filled the stadium everywhere, it is hard to know what to admire most: his resistance, his longevity as a player, or his continued power to attract large crowds.

True, the televised matches of the Brazilian team in the 1970

Mundial made people who until then had taken no interest in sport long to see "in the flesh" the man who had introduced them to the art of soccer.

If we are to believe a Japanese journalist quoted by Ney Bianchi in the Rio magazine *Manchete*, on June 21, 1970 (the day of the Final in Mexico City), Pelé's name was pronounced and written more times in one day than that of any other world-renowned person—living or dead—during the entire period in which they aroused public interest.

While this claim would be difficult to prove, another statement by Ney Bianchi himself seems more acceptable: "Pelé is the most famous Brazilian of all times. He is a world-renowned personality whose name has been written most frequently in all known languages."

Regardless of whether this last claim is excessive or not, it is certain that Pelé's fame has largely exceeded the bounds of the sports world. Significantly, Chiefs of State, the most obvious figures of political power, have been eager to receive him and to treat him with full honors.

These include, of course, the Presidents who have succeeded each other in Brazil from Kubitschek to General Medici. But also Richard Nixon, Robert Kennedy, Gerald Ford, the Queen of England (who insisted on attending one of his matches during an official visit to Rio), the King of Sweden, the heads of several African states, the petroleum kings of the Middle East.

Pelé has kept some colorful memories of his receptions by statesmen in African countries, for example, that of the minister of Gabon, who refused to pay the Santos game guarantee to anybody but Pelé because he wanted to have a private conversation with him in his office.

Or that of the Nigerian Chief of State, a respected patriarch who received Pelé in his palace and gazed at him meditatively as if he were the apparition of the god he had been expecting: "You are Pelé! ... You are Pelé! ..."

In Ryad, King Faisal, a practical man, offered to hire him for a year to do demonstrations for the children in Saudi Arabian schools: "I offer you $30,000 a month, plus a bonus of $400,000 at the time of signing the contract for one year, plus a luxurious residence, plus a big deluxe car with a chauffeur . . ."

Embarrassed, Pelé tried to get out of the situation by jocularly counter-proposing: "$500,000 as bonus for signing and a monthly salary of $40,000 would suit me better . . ."

Taken at his word by the petroleum king, the King of Soccer had to fall back on the contract that bound him to Santos to justify his rejection of these fabulous proposals.

In Europe those in power have showered Pelé with honors and distinctions. After having driven down the Champs-Élysées in an open car to the ovations of the Parisian crowd lining the route in 1971, he was received at City Hall by the municipal council of the capital and a minister of the government. Shortly before, the French government had appointed him Chevalier of the Order of Merit.

When he was received in the Vatican by Pope Paul VI, Pelé, a practicing Catholic, was impressed. According to Brazilian newspaper reports, the Pope said to him: "Don't be nervous! I am more nervous than you, because I have been wanting to meet Pelé personally for a long time!"

No doubt, Pelé owes these official honors to the fact that politicians want to use the most famous soccer player to improve their image with the huge number of sports fans. Indeed, we know that in a great number of countries, and particularly those where dictatorial regimes are in power, soccer is used as an effective instrument of diversion.

But we should not underestimate the feeling of curiosity that must have moved those in power to wish to know this ball player who possesses the extremely rare privilege of worldwide popularity. The same motivation could explain the attraction he has always had for artists. It was not mere chance that a celebrated actress like Brigitte Bardot took part in the festivities on the occasion of his visit to Paris in 1971.

There really is something extraordinary about the unananimous reception and the love shown to Pelé by crowds in all countries.

Predictably Africa, the continent of his ancestors, has offered him the warmest and most spontaneous receptions.

At Libreville, which only has 70,000 inhabitants, 50,000 people were waiting for him at the airport when he came to play in the capital of Gabon.

In the stadium of Kinshasa some years ago, 80,000 Zairians yelled the two syllabes of his name continuously while General Mobutu, holding his hand and looking him straight in the eyes, announced: "The people of the Congo feel honored by the presence in their country of the best soccer player of all times, but also by a man who is respected throughout the entire world!"

After a match in Lagos, the hotel of the Santos player was besieged one evening by an enormous crowd hoping to accompany him to a reception to which he'd been invited by a local society. Tired from the trip and a match in which he had been slightly injured, Pelé excused himself. One of the Santos officials announced this to the crowd at the hotel entrance. But the inhabitants of the Nigerian capital "wanted Pelé," and the demonstration became so unruly that the Brazilian ambassador, called in urgently, tried to explain that the doctor had ordered Pelé to rest in bed. This did not succeed in convincing a gathering that was becoming increasingly irritated. Thousands of voices screamed: "We want Pelé . . . dead or alive!"

This disturbing turn of events made Pelé decide to get up and wave at the crowd from his window for a long time. Threats now gave way to joy. The reporter of the Santos paper, A Tribuna, who relates this incident concludes his article:

"In Black Africa Pelé is a man-god whose name is pronounced as reverently as those of the gods of tribal religions. To rock their children to dreams their mothers tell them the story of Pelé. For millions of beings, children, adolescents, adults, he is the symbol of the advancement of Black people. . . ."

For similar reasons Pelé arouses everywhere—in Europe as in the United States, where all his games fill the stadiums—the admiration and affection of the popular masses who identify with him.

He has often debated on this himself and spoken of it with his intimate friends, such as the Santos journalist to whom he confided:

"Children who never said anything and can't stop talking when they see me, people of all ages who could not walk and run toward me. . . . People who touch my hands or my clothes when I walk by. . . . People who speak languages I don't understand and shout my name. . . . What have I done to provoke such reactions? Why me, when I come from a poor family, have had no education, know that we are all equal and brothers, that people should treat each other as equals, regardless of whether they are rich or poor, famous or unknown? . . . I have never considered myself a superior being. When I was a kid, I used to like to put things together, repair things in the house. I had a real knack for it. . . . But lots of others can do as well. . . . Now I like to play the guitar, sing songs on my own that I compose for fun, go fishing, sometimes cook dishes I like, and especially be at home with my wife and children, where I am not disturbed. I also like to kid around with my pals on the team. . . .

"I am very conscious of being like others. It is only because I manage well when I have a ball at my feet that so many people seem to consider me a being apart?"

Let us try to answer these questions.

13

The Universal Language

For certain moralists the explanation of Pelé's universal popularity can be summed up in a few words. What do people want? Bread and circuses. In case they lack bread, you offer them circus games. And that's where Pelé comes in.

It must be admitted that for several years now soccer has too often offered a picture that justifies contempt if one is concerned about human dignity.

The spectacle of certain games can be degrading: on the playing field, gladiators using every means of cheating, intimidation, and systematic brutality in the presence of a powerless and sometimes frightened referee; in the stands, bullies blinded by chauvinism whistling, shouting, insulting, throwing all sorts of projectiles and firecrackers in order to impress the visiting team, expressing feelings of hate or unjustified satisfaction with the same stupidity ("We've won! We've won!").

Television and the newspapers often try to veil such degrading horrors from the general public or sweep them under the carpet with lenient comments ("They don't mean any harm!") or "technical" justifications ("It's a man's game!"). As for the authorities, they wink at the "necessity for the people to let off steam." After all, isn't soccer a sort of safety valve? One well-known politician admitted cynically: "As long as 'they' get excited about men who fight over a ball, they don't think about making demands or calling things into question."

Soccer becomes a diversion in the service of "national prestige," which is often identified with that of the Chief of State.

As early as 1938, the World Cup held in Italy and won by the team of the organizing country was the pretext for an enormous manifestation of the glory of the "Duce" and his regime.

In 1967 in Buenos Aires, General Ongania, President of the Argentine Republic, beside whom I watched the Intercontinental Final between Racing Buenos Aires and Glasgow Celtic (he had "democratically" taken a seat in the Press Section), declared at the end of the game: "The Argentine players have filled me with pride!"

They had won the match. But how?

By terrorizing, by cowardly massacring the Scottish players, who are not known for being softies, with the active participation of 80,000 "supporters" and the obvious complicity of the referee who had decided to opt for the only means that would enable him to get out of the arena unharmed.

A few minutes before the game, while the players were warming up on the field, a stone thrown from the stands closest to the Scots hit their goalkeeper on the head. He was carried off to the dressing rooms bleeding and unconscious.

That was only the prelude to a series of aggressions committed against the Scottish players from the kickoff to the end of the game. Aggressions that were manifestly premeditated and almost always perpetrated against players far from the ball, that is, from the referee's view; but visible to the spectators in the stands, who applauded and encouraged them, and to the linesmen who did not dare call them to the attention of the referee.

Thanks to a goal scored so illegally that nobody could fail to notice it, Racing Buenos Aires made off with a victory which aroused the indignation of the entire foreign press and of numerous Argentine journalists, sickened by the hideous parody which had filled the Chief of State with such pride.

A few days later I asked Jock Stein, the technical director of Celtic, why he had not ordered his team to leave the field when his goalkeeper Simpson was evacuated on a stretcher with his head bleeding and it appeared certain that the game could not be played under normal conditions. He replied: "That was my intention, but then I thought, if we did that, the crowd would lynch us."

No doubt Stein was right, for there have sometimes been deaths in the stands of the big stadiums that could not be attributed to emotions caused by the game but were due to scuffles or mass panic provoked by the explosion of chauvinistic passions. The horrible catastrophe in the National Stadium in Lima which killed 300 persons and caused several thousand injuries is the saddest and most famous example one can cite to illustrate the consequences of this deterioration of the spirit surrounding the game.

Incidents of this sort are fortunately quite rare, but even when no blood flows, a good many crimes are committed each week in every country in the name of soccer.

The ever-increasing importance of money in the big competitions, and the growing utilization of athletic victories for political ends under the banner of national prestige, are the main reasons for this degeneration of soccer; little by little it extends to the amateurs, ever ready to follow the example from so high above.

Once the facts have been recognized, an analysis of their causes and remedies should be a task for the "moralists"—and a proper test of their intellectual honesty. But they prefer to cry shame and pay no further attention to an activity that involves a considerable number of human beings, most of them young, whose well-being certainly ought to be their concern.

Would it really be too difficult objectively to analyze all the aspects of soccer as a social phenomenon, or at any rate the methods required to find the key to this other phenomenon—the universal fame and popularity of Pelé?

Soccer is not a fashion, a passing fad. It was born in England more than a century ago, and has been implanted gradually in every country on every continent. Like all living organisms, it has received the stamp of the climatic, geographic, economic, historical, and social conditions peculiar to the various environments in which its development has occurred. (Hence the fascination of international encounters which demonstrate the clash of the very different styles of play fashioned by such factors.)

Soccer has experienced an impressive quantitative increase (the International Federation, FIFA, with headquarters in Zurich, controls 141 nations—more than the United Nations). The joining of federations from countries that have recently become independent does not by itself explain the extension of such an empire, built with the help of two Frenchmen: Robert Guérin, who conceived the idea and laid the first cornerstone in 1904; and Jules Rimet, who constructed the edifice from 1921 to 1954 and gave it its most beautiful ornament, the World Cup, open to all nations.

In spite of the obstacles encountered by practitioners of soccer with the disappearance of open spaces in big towns, soccer has not ceased to gain new adherents in the industrial nations. The number of licensed players in Europe has increased from 8 million in 1966 to 15 million in 1973. And in order to get a more adequate idea of the real number of participants, we must add the millions of players from high school, university, industrial, and affiliated federations in which FIFA and continental confederations, such as the Union Européenne de Football Association (UEFA), show no interest. On top of this we would have to include "sandlot soccer" as played in competitions involving factories, workshops, and offices—competitions that are particularly numerous in the spring.

One can get some idea of the relative strength of European countries by noting that West Germany has the greatest number of licensed players, with 3,500,000, followed closely by the U.S.S.R., then Great Britain, and France—which, contrary to widely accepted opinion, is one of the top soccer nations in the world so far as the number of participants is concerned (1 million officially recorded in 1974).

It is more difficult to evaluate the number of soccer players in South America. If we limit ourselves to the figures supplied by the Brazilian Confederation of Sports, Brazil would only have

75,000 amateur players. The comparison with the figure of 18
million quoted a few years ago by the daily *A Gazeta Esportive*
of Sao Paulo brings out an anomaly that can easily be explained.
In Brazil, as in all countries of South America, Africa, and south-
ern Europe, the real number of players bears no relation to the
number of licenses issued by the federations.

In Brazil, as in Africa (more so than in Spain and Italy), all
the young play or have played soccer, and almost all the adults
have played it. All observations, all inquiries prove this point. In
the countries that have recently taken to soccer but traditionally
assign much importance to the administrative aspect of organization, the number of licensed players does give an exact idea of
quantitative developments. In a few years Australia, a latecomer
to soccer, has attained the figure of 200,000 practitioners.

While it is not my intention here to pile up statistics, it is
important to note that at present the number of players throughout the world who engage in soccer on a regular basis is evalu-
ated at more than 30 million. If we were to add up the
participants in all other sports, we would not arrive at one-half of
this figure.

The mass of people who are interested in or get excited about
soccer without practicing it is still more important. All of this
opens up interesting perspectives for the development of the
sport, despite the shortage of playing fields, the indifference of
the authorities to the needs of the young, the limited number of
years the average career of a soccer player can last, and the
sometimes questionable attraction of a game turned into a carica-
ture by those who ought to be its best promoters.

Contrary to what certain people who despise sports imagine,
soccer spectators always play an active part in the game—an
unhealthy and odious part when they turn into chauvinistic supporters. But it is a positive one when they take a passionate
interest in the game itself, for their influence on the players
whom they inspire and incite to surpass themselves is so obvious
that one cannot imagine a high-class match without the participation of an excited crowd.

Rather than delve into statistics to give an idea of the importance of soccer spectators, let us limit ourselves to some salient examples.

The 1970 World Cup Games in Mexico were watched by more than 1,500,000 spectators, which amounts to an average of 50,000 per game.

The European Champions' Cup has drawn each season a total on average of 2,500,000 spectators, and the European Cup Winners' Cup, 1,500,000.

In England, the professional championship competition, which consists of four divisions, is attended every year by 30 million spectators.

In West Germany, for the First Division alone, more than 6,500,000 pass through the turnstiles. In France, some 4 million.

To obtain an overall view of the total number of spectators of soccer matches in each country, we would have to count those at amateur matches, too. And obviously if we are measuring the full extent of important games, the number of TV viewers would also have to be included. Surveys undertaken by the TV rating specialists are fairly accurate and enable us to state that the World Cup Final in Mexico City was watched by nearly 1 billion spectators!

Now let us cite the results of an inquiry made in 1969 by the magazine *Veja* about the interest in "futebol" among the various social categories in Brazil's population.

According to this inquiry, 86 percent of the workers, 88 percent of the middle class, 95 percent of the students, and 72 percent of the women are soccer fans. Among them, 45 percent prefer watching games in the stadium and only 17 percent on television. Some 72 percent of the men questioned were playing or had played soccer. *Veja*—which is not a sports magazine, a fact that should be noted—entitles its article: "The Sport of Almost Everyone."

Although it is true that in Brazil the passion for soccer is a more important phenomenon than anywhere else, nobody can deny that this passion constitutes a universal fact. One may regret that soccer involves considerable economic interests, but it should not be forgotten that this is an inevitable evolution in a society based on the exchange of goods and services.

Being an athletic activity but also a spectacle, soccer adopts the form sof "industrial" organization. In England the professional clubs have since the turn of the century been stock corporations, managed like real commercial enterprises. And while professional soccer has not taken on the same forms in all countries, the notion of financial viability, frequently set forth in a very explicit manner, is used as the justification for measures whose effect on the club's behavior on the field is important.

By now it is recognized everywhere that soccer at the highest level is a business which involves considerable financial interests. Directly in the form of receipts, the salaries of the players, of technical and administrative personnel, the cost of the transfer of players; indirectly by the effect of the trips and lodging of players and fans on the transport business, the hotel business, local merchants, and so on. It serves no purpose to tabulate the precise figures the specialized press publishes on receipts as if they were victories. Suffice it to point out that the mere sale of tickets for the 1970 World Cup in Mexico produced as net gain (after taxes) the colossal sum of $6.5 million for thirty-two games played in that competition.

"The football industry," as it was called as early as 1951 in a publication by the London Political and Economic Planning Board, is certainly not a figment of the imagination. If I cite it as an objective fact, I do so to show the place that soccer as a social phenomenon occupies in the modern world.

Once this has been demonstrated, we need to examine what gave birth to this phenomenon, justified its development, and conditions its future.

Soccer is not a modern version of the ball games that were played, as the textbooks tell us, before our era in China, then in ancient Greece, and later in Italy and France during the Middle Ages.

Its birth is far more recent. It took place in England in the middle of the nineteenth century in the initial period of the rise of big industry. Its creation was in no way fortuitous, but responded to specific needs.

First of all, a physical need: that of workers immobilized for long hours at their machines and naturally longing to get out into the open air in order to make the inactive muscles of their lower body function, since their work called essentially on the muscles of their upper body. This explains the form of the sport invented by the English workers: a game that would exercise the muscles of their legs in movements and runs carried out on a field of large dimensions for the control, conduct, and shooting of a ball heavy enough to require strength.

The social function of its inventors also explains the content they gave to their sport: its team spirit. The division of labor in the factory makes the worker conscious of the fact that he supplies an essential contribution to the collective work. It is natural that he will inject into the game he has freely chosen the conception born of his daily work and developed by him. The objective in this game—to produce goals—can thus only be the result of collective action, with the ball constituting the instrument that represents the link among the team members.

In soccer, as in the factory, there is a division of tasks: that of the goalkeeper is by definition different from that of the center forward. But there is nevertheless a fundamental difference between work and play. In soccer, specialization (except for the goalkeeper, the only player who can use his hands within the limits of the penalty area) does not imply that a player may not participate in other tasks: the fullback can attack and score goals, the forward can come to the aid of his defenders; even the goalkeeper can make an important contribution to offensive construction by accurate passes.

In soccer the player is not a piece of machinery as in factory work. He is a man capable of individual initiative, of innovation, of original creation.

The player in possession of the ball is the absolute master of play. He determines the movement into position of his partners as well as of his opponents. His power is a temporary one, for he will give up the ball either voluntarily for the benefit of a partner or involuntarily for the benefit of an opponent. But in the course of the game he will find himself several times in this position of power and he will exercise it fully.

The necessity for each player to show his spirit of initiative, his freedom of choice, his intelligence is, moreover, a permanent feature of the game. Even when he does not have the ball, his position play and his movements oblige him to use his brains.

Thus soccer responds to the legitimate aspiration of every human being: to communicate freely with others, to participate voluntarily with them in the accomplishment of a task in such a way that the profit is returned to the collectivity he has adopted and which has adopted him—the team.

For these reasons, one can understand its attraction for young workers and also for young people and adults belonging to the most disadvantaged social classes who, by the nature of their work (or absence of work), are deprived of all expression, communication, or participation.

Even among the ruling classes—which often try to use the infatuation of the popular masses for soccer for their own ends—there are many who, more or less consciously, seek in the practice or spectacle of soccer a conception of human relationships which differs from that reflected in the organization of society.

The philosophy and morality of individual sports are indeed diametrically opposed to those of soccer. For the trackman, the boxer, the golfer, the skier, or the tennis player, it is a question of asserting himself individually at the detriment of others, of proving the superiority of his "ego" over that of others.

This philosophy and this morality could not fulfill the aspirations of the majority of men, even though they may temporarily satisfy the will for power of some.

Despite the ballyhoo artificially created for commercial reasons, as in boxing matches, or for reasons of national prestige, as in the Olympic Games, the development of individual sports,

even with the aid that many governments furnish them, cannot
bear comparison with that of soccer.

The reason is that the language invented by the English
workers of the nineteenth century, and later codified by the intellectuals who formulated the Laws of the Information Board, has
become a universal language. It is as well understood and used in
Peking as in Manaus, in Djakarta as in Leningrad, in Toronto as
in Caracas, in Sydney as in Timbuktu.

And it is perfectly normal that the greatest popularity should
be enjoyed by those who speak this language best, the teams and
the players whose performances place them at the top of the
hierarchy of values. Herein lies the key to Pelé's universal renown.

In order for this language that he used as a master to be
understood by all, there first had to be people everywhere in a
position to have a technical knowledge of the game, in other
words, practitioners and knowledgeable spectators. This implied
a certain degree of development in the game and of means of
audiovisual information.

But the fact (noticed by numerous observers) that so many
women, children, and people of all ages usually indifferent to
sport were so deeply impressed by Pelé's performance when they
saw him for the first time in the 1970 World Cup, thanks to
television, cannot be attributed to technical competence.

Could not this phenomenon be explained as a kind of intuitive awareness of the harmonious conception of life which soccer
contains, when individual genius places itself at the service of a
collectivity as naturally and completely as Pelé did during that
World Cup?

If we examine the principal aspects of Pelé's personality that
emerge from the analysis of his life as a man and as an artist, we
notice that all the circumstances seem to have combined in such
a way as to make soccer his means of expression.

His atavism endowed him with a particular aptitude for expressing himself by gesture and movement. The poverty of his

family deprived him of immediate access to the means of traditional abstract or artistic communication. His spontaneous passion for soccer was encouraged by his father in spite of the vexations the latter's own career had caused him. His aggressiveness, maintained by the necessities of the struggle for life, was tempered by maternal gentleness. His health and physical vitality were those of a vigorous product of natural selection. His quickness of mind had thousands of occasions to become sharpened in those matches in the street or on sandlots where cleverness is indispensable. And his genius found favorable conditions for breaking through and flowering in a period in which soccer was still an art.

As an adult he was attracted by music, that other universal language. But while he has composed some melancholy songs in the calm atmosphere of training retreats and though he sings them sometimes for close friends, he has never been, like his teammates in the national selection—Jairzinho and Brito—a samba virtuoso, that popular Brazilian art which combines music and dance.

And because he possesses in the highest degree the faculty to "transmit to others his feelings . . . by means of certain exterior signs," Pelé has been understood and loved by the world. That is the secret of his universal popularity.

A secret that the Americans, who until now have turned a deaf ear to the language of soccer, are about to discover, if we are to judge by Larry Merchant's editorial column in the New York *Post* of June 19, 1975, where the writer attempts to explain Pelé's power of attraction on American crowds:

He is Babe Ruth and the Rolling Stones, and Billy Graham in one dynamic box-office package. He could sell out Siberia.

Reason being that he speaks an international language, drawn into the marrow from the cradle, and soccer is the most popular game on earth.

No wonder a Brazilian exclaimed: "We shall have to wait two centuries before another Pelé emerges!"

APPENDIXES

Pelé's Visiting Card

- World Cup 1958, 1962, and 1970.
- Intercontinental Cup 1962 and 1963.
- South American Cup of Clubs 1961 and 1962.
- Brazilian Cup 1968.
- Sao Paulo Championship 1958, 1960, 1961, 1962, 1964, 1967, 1968, and 1974.
- Rio–Sao Paulo Tournament 1959, 1961, 1963, 1964, and 1966.

Distinguishing Marks

- The only winner of three World Cups.
- The youngest world champion (seventeen in 1958).
- Top scorer of the Sao Paulo League for ten consecutive years: 1957 through 1966. Won this title again in 1974.
- The first Black athlete to have his picture on the cover of *Life*.
- The first soccer player to have scored more than 1,000 goals in his professional career.

Pelé's Four World Cups

1958
8th Final
Brazil beats U.S.S.R. 2–0

Goals: Vava (2).
Brazil: Gilmar - De Sordi, Bellini, Orlando, N. Santos - Didi, Zito - Garrincha, Vava, Pelé, Zagalo.

U.S.S.R.: Yachine - Kassarev, Krijewski, Kusnetzov, Tzarev - Voinov, Netto - A. Ivanov, V. Ivanov, Simonian, Iliyne.

Quarter-final
Brazil beats Wales 1–0

Goal: Pelé.

Brazil: Gilmar - De Sordi, Bellini, Orlando, N. Santos - Didi, Zito - Garrincha, Mazzola, Pelé, Zagalo.

Wales: Kelsey - Williams, M. Charles, Hopkins - Sullivan, Bowen - Medwin, Hewitt, Webster, Allchurch, Jones.

Semi-final
Brazil beats France 5–2

Goals: Vava, Didi, Pelé (3), Fontaine, Piantoni.

Brazil: Gilmar - De Sordi, Bellini, Orlando, N. Santos - Didi, Zito - Garrincha, Vava, Pelé, Zagalo.

France: Abbès - Kaelbel, Jonquet, Lerond-Penverne, Marcel - Wisnieski, Fontaine, Kopa, Piantoni, Vincent.

Final
Brazil beats Sweden 5–2

Goals: Vava (2), Pelé (2), Zagalo, Liedholm, Simonsson.

Brazil: Gilmar - D. Santos, Bellini, Orlando, N. Santos - Didi, Zito - Garrincha, Vava, Pelé, Zagalo.

Sweden: Svensson - Bergmark, Bustavsson, Axbom - Bœrjœsson, Parling - Hamrin, Gren, Simonsson, Liedholm, Skoglund.

1962
8th Final
Brazil beats Mexico 2–0

Goals: Zagalo, Pelé.

Brazil: Gilmar - D. Santos, Mauro, Zozimo, N. Santos - Didi, Zito - Garrincha, Vava, Pelé, Zagalo.

Mexico: Carbajal - Del Muro, Cardenas, Sepulveda, Villegas - Najera, Jasso - Del Aguila, Reyes, Hernandez, Diaz.

Brazil and Czechoslovakia 0–0

Brazil: Gilmar - D. Santos, Mauro, Zozimo, N. Santos - Didi, Zito - Garrincha, Vava, Pelé, Zagalo.
Czechoslovakia: Schroiff - Lala, Pluskal, Popluhar, Novak - Scherer, Masopust - Stibranyi, Kvasniak, Adamek, Jellinek.

1966
8th Final
Brazil beats Bulgaria 2–0

Goals: Pelé, Garrincha.
Brazil: Gilmar - D. Santos, Bellini, Altair, P. Enrique - Lima, Denilson - Garrincha, Alcindo, Pelé, Jaïrzinho.
Bulgaria: Naidenov - Chalamanov, Penev, Voustov, Gaganelov - Kitov, Jetchev - Dermendiev, Asparoukhov, Yakimov, Kolev.

Portugal beats Brazil 3–1

Goals: Eusebio (2), Simœs, Rildo.
Portugal: J. Pereira - Morais, Batista, Vicente, Hilario - Coluna, Graça - Augusto, Eusebio, Torrès, Simœs.
Brazil: Manga - Fidelis, Brito, Orlando, Rildo - Lima, Denilson - Jairzinho, Silva, Pelé, Parana.

1970
Eliminations
Brazil beats Colombia 2–0 (in Bogota)

Goals: Tostao (2).
Brazil: Felix - Carlos Alberto, D. Dias, Joel, Rildo - Piazza, Gerson - Jaïrzinho (Paul Cesar), Tostao, Pelé, Edu.

Brazil beats Venezuela 5–0 (in Caracas)

Goals: Tostao (3), Pelé (2).
Brazil: Felix - Carlos Alberto, D. Dias, Joel, Rildo (Everaldo) - Piazza, Gerson - Jaïrzinho, Tostao, Pelé, Edu.

Brazil beats Paraguay 3–0 (in Asuncion)

Goals: Jaïrzinho, Edu, Mendoza (self-goal).
Brazil: Felix - Carlos Albert, Dias, Joel, Rildo - Piazza, Gerson - Jaïrzinho, Tostao, Pelé, Edu.

Brazil beats Colombia 6–2 (in Rio)

Goals: Tostao (2), Edu, Pelé, Rivelino, Jaïrzinho.
Brazil: Felix - Carlos Alberto, Dias, Joel, Rildo - Piazza, Gerson (Rivelino) - Jaïrzinho, Tostao, Pelé (Paulo Cesar), Edu.

Brazil beats Venezuela 6–0 (in Rio)

Goals: Tostao (3), Pelé (2), Jaïrzinho.
Brazil: Felix (Lula) - Carlos Albert, Dias, Joel (Brito), Rildo - Piazza, Gerson - Jaïrzinho, Tostao, Pelé, Edu.

Brazil beats Paraguay 1–0 (in Maracana)

Goal: Pelé.
Brazil: Felix - Carlos Alberto, Dias, Joel, Rildo - Piazza, Gerson - Jaïrzinho, Tostao, Pelé, Edu.

8th Final
Brazil beats Czechoslovakia: 4–1 (1-1)

80,000 spectators. Referee: Mr. Baretto Ruiz (Uruguay).
Goals: Petras (11') for Czechoslovakia, Rivelino (23'), Pelé (60') and Jaïrzinho (67' and 83') for Brazil.
Brazil: Felix - Carlos Alberto, Brito, Piazza, Everaldo - Gerson (Paulo Cesar), Clodoaldo - Jaïrzinho, Tostao, Pelé, Rivelino.
Czechoslovakia: Viktor - Dobias, Horvath, Migas, Hagara - Kuna, Hrdlicka (Kvasniak) - Frantisek Vesely, Petras, Adamec, Jokl.

Brazil beats England: 1–0 (0–0)

80,000 spectators. Referee: Mr. Klein (Israel).
Goal: Jaïrzinho (59').
Brazil: Felix - Carlos Alberto, Brito, Piazza, Everaldo - Paulo Cesar, Clodoaldo - Jaïrzinho, Pelé, Tostao (Roberto), Rivelino.
Angleterre: Banks - Wright, Labone, Moore, Cooper - Mullery, Charlton (Astle), Peters - Lee (Bell), Ball, Hurst.

Brazil beats Rumania: 3–2 (2–0)

20,000 spectators. Referee: Mr. Marshall (Austria).
Goals: Pelé (19' and 65'), Jaïrzinho (20') for Brazil. Dumitrache (34') and Dembrowski (82') for Rumania.
Brazil: Felix - Carlos Alberto, Brito, Fontana, Everaldo (Marco An-

tonio) - Clodoaldo (Edu), Piazza, Paulo Cesar - Jaïrzinho, Tostao, Pelé.

Rumania: Adamache (Raducanu) - Satmareanu, Dinu, Lupescu, Mocanu - Dembrowski, Dumitru, Nunweiller - Neagu, Dumitrache (Tataru), Lucescu.

Quarter-final
Brazil beats Peru: 4–2 (2–1)

50,000 spectators. Referee: Mr. Loraux (Belgium).

Goals: Rivelino (11'), Tostao (15' and 52') Jaïrzinho (77') for Brazil. Gallardo (27') and Cubillas (69') for Peru.

Brazil: Felix - Carlos Alberto, Brito, Piazza, Everaldo (Marco Antonio) - Clodoaldo, Gerson (Paulo Cesar) - Jaïrzinho, Tostao, Pelé, Rivelino.

Peru: Rubinos - Campos, Fernandez, Chumpitaz, Fuentès - Mifflin, Challe - Cubillas, Baylon (Sotil), Perico Leon, Gallardo.

Semi-final
Brazil beats Uruguay: 3–1 (1–1)

60,000 spectators. Referee: Mr. Ortiz de Mendibil (Spain).

Goals: Clodoaldo (45e), Jaïrzinho (75e), Rivelino (89e) for Brazil. Cubilla (18e) for Uruguay.

Brazil: Felix - Carlos Alberto, Brito, Piazza, Everaldo - Clodoaldo, Gerson - Jaïrzinho, Tostao, Pelé, Rivelino.

Uruguay: Mazurkiewicz - Ubinas, Ancheta, Matosas, Mujica - Cortès, Monteiro, Maneiro (Esparrago) - Cubilla, Fontès, Moralès.

Final
Brazil beats Italy: 4–1 (1–1)

110,000 spectators. Referee: Mr. Gloeckner (East Germany).

Goals: Pelé (17e), Gerson (66e), Jaïrzinho (71e), Carlos Alberto (87e) for Brazil. Boninsegna (37e) for Italy.

Brazil: Felix - Carlos Alberto, Brito, Piazza, Everaldo - Clodoaldo, Gerson - Jaïrzinho, Tostao, Pelé, Rivelino.

Italy: Albertosi - Cera - Burgnich, Rosato, Bertini (Juliano), Faccheti - Mazzola, De Sisti - Domenghini, Boninsegna (Rivera), Riva.

Pelé's 1,000 Goals

(From his first professional game on September 7, 1956 until the match SANTOS–VASCO DA GAMA on November 19, 1969, the official list of Pelé's 1,000 goals as published in the Brazilian press.)

1956

9 - 7 — Santos, 7 - Corintians de Santo André, 1	1
11 - 15 — Santos, 4 - Jabaquara, 2	1

1957

3 - 24 — Santos, 3 - Guarani de Bagé, 5	1
3 - 31 — Santos, 4 - Juventus, 1	1
4 - 14 — Santos, 5 - Guarani de Campinas, 3	2
4 - 11 — Santos, 6 - Corintians Paulista, 1	2
4 - 26 — Santos, 3 - Sao Paulo, 1	1
5 - 15 — Santos, 3 - Palmeiras, 0	2
5 - 19 — Santos, 7 - Londrina, 1	2
5 - 29 — Santos, 4 - América do Rio, 0	1
6 - 2 — Santos, 2 - Vasco de Gama, 3	1
6 - 9 — Santos, 7 - Lavras, 2	4
6 - 19 — Santos-Vasco, 6 - Belenenses, 1	3
6 - 22 — Santos-Vasco, 1 - Dinamo, 1	1
6 - 25 — Santos-Vasco, 1 - Flamengo, 1	1
7 - 1 —Santos-Vasco, 1 - Sao Paulo, 1	1
7 - 7 — Brazil, 1 - Argentina, 2	1
7 - 10 — Brazil, 2 - Argentina, 0	1
7 - 14 — Santos, 5 - XV Piracicaba, 3	1
7 - 23 — Santos, 3 - Benfica Lisbon, 2	1
7 - 25 — Santos, 7 - Ponte Preta, 2	3
8 - 15 — Santos, 8 - Guarani de Campinas, 1	4
9 - 8 — Santos, 1 - Palmeiras, 2	1
9 - 11 — Santos, 7 - Nacional, 1	4
9 - 15 — Santos, 2 - Sao Paulo, 3	1
9 - 22 — Santos, 1 - AA Portuguêsa, 1	1
9 - 25 — Santos, 9 - Ipiranga, 1	3
9 - 29 — Santos, 6 - Juventus, 1	1
10 - 6 — Santos, 2 - Sampaio Moreira (Maranhao), 1	2

10 - 8 — Santos, 2 - Recife 1 1
10 - 26 — Santos, 4 - Palmeiras, 3 1
11 - 3 — Santos, 3 - Corintians Paulista, 3 3
11 - 10 — Santos, 3 - XV de Piracicaba, 0 1
11 - 24 — Santos, 5 - Jabaquara, 1 3
11 - 27 — Santos, 6 - XV de Piracicaba, 2 2
12 - 1 — Santos, 6 - AA Portuguêsa, 2 4
12 - 8 — Santos, 2 - Ponte Preta, 1 1
12 - 15 — Santos, 6 - Portuguêsa de Desportos, 0 2
12 - 29 — Santos, 10 - Nitro-Quimica, 3 1

1958

1 - 16 — Santos, 4 - Bragantino, 1 1
1 - 26 — Santos, 4 - Prudentina, 0 1
1 - 30 — Santos, 2 - Atlético Mineiro, 5 1
2 - 2 — Santos, 2 - Atlético Mineiro, 0 1
7 - 2 — Santos, 4 - Botafogo (Rib. Prêto), 2 1
2 - 26 — Santos, 5 - América Rio, 3 4
3 - 6 — Santos, 7 - Palmeiras, 6 1
3 - 9 — Santos, 2 - Flamengo, 3 1
3 - 13 — Santos, 2 - Portuguêsa de Desportos, 3 1
3 - 27 — Santos, 1 - Corintians Paulista, 2 1
5 - 4 — Brazil, 5 - Paraguay, 1 1
5 - 18 — Brazil, 3 - Bulgària, 0 2
6 - 19 — Brazil, 1 - Wales, 0 1
6 - 24 — Brazil, 5 - France, 2 3
6 - 29 — Brazil, 5 - Sweden, 2 2
7 - 16 — Santos, 7 - Jabaquara, 3 2
7 - 20 — Santos, 2 - Juventus, 1 1
7 - 23 — Santos, 6 - XV de Piracicaba, 0 4
7 - 27 — Santos, 2 - Botafogo (Rib. Prêto), 2 2
7 - 31 — Santos, 1 - Commercial, 1 1
8 - 5 — Santos, 4 - Portuguêsa de Desportos, 3 1
8 - 13 — Santos, 4 - Ferroviàra, 3 1
8 - 17 — Santos, 1 - Sao Paulo, 0 1
8 - 20 — Santos, 4 - Ponte Prêta, 0 1
8 - 28 — Santos, 5 - XV de Jau, 2 1

9 - 4 — Santos, 3 - Taubaté, 0	1
9 - 11 — Santos, 10 - Nacional, 0	4
9 - 14 — Santos, 1 - Corintians Paulista, 0	1
9 - 17 — Santos, 8 - Guarani de Campinas, 1	1
9 - 21 — Santos, 2 - Prudentina, 2	1
9 - 25 — Santos, 8 - Ipiranga, 1	5
10 - 15 — Santos, 6 - AA Portuguêsa, 1	3
10 - 19 — Santos, 5 - XV de Piracicaba, 0	2
10 - 22 — Santos, 6 - Jabaquara, 2	3
10 - 26 — Santos, 4 - Botafogo (Rib. Prêto), 0	3
11 - 5 — Santos, 3 - América (Rio Prêto), ...	1
11 - 16 — Santos, 2 - Palmeiras, 1	1
11 - 19 — Santos, 9 - Commercial (Rib. Prêto), 1	4
11 - 27 — Santos, 2 - AA Portuguêsa, 1	1
11 - 30 — Santos, 4 - Nacional, 3	1
12 - 7 — Santos, 6 - Corintians, 1	4
12 - 10 — Santos, 7 - Juventus, 1	3
12 - 14 — Santos, 7 - Guarani, 1	4
12 - 18 — Santos, 2 - Sao Paulo, 2	2
12 - 21 — Santos, 1 - Coritiba, 1	1
12 - 23 — Santos, 4 - Cruzeiro, 2	3
12 - 30 — Santos, 3 - Combinado Paulista, 0	2

1959

4 - 1 — Santos, 3 - Sport Boys (Peru), 0	2
1 - 6 — Santos, 4 - Sporting Cristal (Peru), 0	2
1 - 11 — Santos, 3 - Emelec (Equador), 1	2
1 - 15 — Santos, 3 - Saprisa (Costa Rica), 1	2
1 - 13 — Santos, 2 - Comunicaciones (Guatemala), 1	1
1 - 21 — Santos, 2 - Sel. Costa Rica, 1	1
1 - 29 — Santos, 4 - Guadalajara (México), 2	3
2 - 8 — Santos, 4 - Atlas (México), 1	2
2 - 12 — Santos, 5 - América (México), 0	2
3 - 10 — Brazil, 2 - Peru, 2	1
3 - 15 — Brazil, 3 - Chile, 0	2
3 - 21 — Brazil, 3 - Bolivia, 2	1
4 - 9 — Santos, 4 - Botafogo (Rio), 2	1

3 - 29 — Brazil, 4 - Paraguay, 1 3
4 - 4 — Brazil, 1 - Argentina, 1 1
4 - 12 — Santos, 3 - Flamengo, 2 1
4 - 26 — Santos, 4 - Sao Paulo, 3 2
4 - 30 — Santos, 3 - Corintians, 2 1
5 - 17 — Santos, 3 - Vasco, 0 1
5 - 19 — Santos, 5 - Santa Cruz, 1 2
5 - 23 — Santos, 3 - Bulgaria "B" Team, 3 2
5 - 25 — Santos, 2 - Bulgaria "A" Team, 0 1
5 - 27 — Santos, 4 - Anderlecht (Belgium), 2 2
6 - 3 — Santos, 3 - Feyehoord (Holland), 0 1
6 - 5 — Santos, 2 - Internazionale (Italy), 3 3
6 - 6 — Santos, 6 - Fortune (Germany), 4 1
6 - 9 — Santos, 4 - Servette (Switzerland), 1 1
6 - 11 — Santos, 6 - Comb. Hamburg (Germany), 0 1
6 - 13 — Santos, 7 - Niedersachsen (Germany), 1 2
6 - 14 — Santos, 5 - Enschede (Holland), 0 3
6 - 17 — Santos, 3 - Real Madrid, 5 1
6 - 19 — Santos, 2 - Sporting, 2 2
6 - 21 — Santos, 4 - Botafogo (in Spain), 1 1
6 - 24 — Santos, 4 - Valencia, 4 1
6 - 26 — Santos, 7 - Internazionale (Italy), 1 4
6 - 28 — Santos, 5 - Barcelona, 1 2
7 - 5 — Santos, 2 - Betis, 2 1
7 - 18 — Santos, 2 - Fortaleza (Ceara), 2 2
7 - 23 — Santos, 7 - Jabaquara, 0 1
7 - 26 — Santos, 8 - XV de Jau, 2 3
8 - 2 — Santos, 4 - Juventus, 0 3
8 - 16 — Santos, 1 - Taubaté, 1 1
8 - 21 — Army, 9 - Policia Portuaria, 0 3
8 - 23 — Santos, 4 - Noroeste, 3 3
8 - 26 — Santos, 3 - Corintians 2 1
8 - 27 — Army, 7 - 2. o. R. M., 0 3
8 - 30 — Santos, 3 - América, 2 1
9 - 7 — Santos, 5 - Portuguésa Desportos, 0 3
9 - 10 — Santos, 4 - Guarani, 1 2
9 - 11 — Army, 8 - Misto Santos, 4 3
9 - 13 — Santos, 3 - Botafogo (Rib. Prêto), 1 1
9 - 17 — Brazil, 7 - Chile, 0 3

9 - 28 — Army, 4 - Forças Armadas, 2 1
10 - 3 — Santos, 7 - Palmeiras, 3 3
10 - 6 — Army, 3 - 2. o. S.E.N., 2 1
10 - 14 — Santos, 8 - América (Rio Prêto), 0 4
10 - 25 — Santos, 5 - XV de Piracicaba, 2 2
10 - 27 — Army, 6 - Marinha, 1 3
11 - 1 — Santos, 6 - Comercial, 2 1
11 - 4 — Santos, 4 - Comercial (Capital), 2 1
11 - 11 — Santos, 5 - Juventus, 1 2
11 - 15 — Santos, 4 - Nacional, 0 2
11 - 22 — Santos, 5 - Portuguêsa de Desportos, 1 3
11 - 23 — Santos, 1 - Palmeiras, 5 1
12 - 6 — Santos, 5 - Ferroviara, 2 2
12 - 9 — Santos, 2 - Bahia, 3 1
12 - 13 — Santos, 4 - Sao Paulo, 2 2
12 - 27 — Santos, 4 - Corintians, 1 2
12 - 30 — Santos, 4 - Bahia, 0 1

1960

1 - 5 — Santos, 1 - Palmeiras, 1 1
10 - 1 — Santos, 1 - Palmeiras, 2 1
3 - 6 — Santos, 3 - Deportivo (Colombia), 1 1
3 - 13 — Santos, 4 - Deportivo (Colombia), 0 1
5 - 1 — Brazil, 3 - RAU. 1 3
5 - 8 — Brazil, 7 - Malmœ, 1 2
5 - 12 — Brazil, 2 - Internazionale, 2 2
5 - 19 — Santos, 4 - Royal Standard (Belgium), 3 3
5 - 25 — Santos, 5 - Polish All-Stars, 2 2
5 - 27 — Santos, 9 - Munich (Germany), 1 3
5 - 28 — Santos, 6 - Anderlecht, 0 2
5 - 31 — Santos, 10 - Beerschot (Belguim), 1 5
6 - 1 — Santos, 3 - Roma, 2 1
6 - 7 — Santos, 5 - Reims (France), 3 2
6 - 9 — Santos, 4 - Racing (France), 1 1
6 - 11 — Santos, 5 - Gantoise (Belgium), 2 2
6 - 15 — Santos, 4 - Berlin All-Stars, 2 1
6 - 16 — Santos, 4 - Eintrach (Germany), 2 2

6 - 17 — Santos, 3 - Reims (France), 1 1
6 - 23 — Santos, 3 - Toulouse (France), 0 2
7 - 2 — Santos, 3 - Barcelone, 4 1
7 - 9 — Brazil, 5 - Uruguay, 1 1
7 - 17 — Santos, 6 - Ponte Preta, 3 1
7 - 27 — Santos, 8 - Jabaquara, 3 3
7 - 31 — Santos, 1 - Corintians, 1 1
8 - 3 — Santos, 5 - Botafogo (Rib. Prêto), 1 1
8 - 10 — Santos, 4 - Noroeste, 1 3
8 - 14 — Santos, 1 - Corintians (P. Prudente), 0 1
8 - 15 — Santos, 3 - Itau, 2 1
8 - 21 — Santos, 3 - Palmeiras, 1 1
9 - 15 — Santos, 5 - Juventus, 2 3
9 - 24 — Santos, 3 - Juventus, 1 2
9 - 28 — Santos, 3 - Portuguêsa Desportos, 4 1
10 - 23 — Santos, 4 - Ponte Preta, 1 1
11 - 6 — Santos, 2 - XV de piracicaba, 0 2
11 - 9 — Santos, 1 - AA Portuguêsa, 0 1
11 - 14 — Santos, 3 - Noroeste, 1 2
11 - 20 — Santos, 4 - Botafogo (Rib. Prêto), 2 1
11 - 23 — Santos, 5 - Corintians (P. Prudente), 0 1
11 - 30 — Santos, 6 - Corintians, 1 1
12 - 4 — Santos, 6 - Taubaté, 1 2
12 - 7 — Santos, 5 - Ferroviara, 0 3
12 - 16 — Santos, 2 - Palmeiras, 1 1

1961

1 - 8 — Santos, 6 - Uberlândia, 1 2
1 - 11 — Santos, 10 - Guarini, 2 2
1 - 14 — Santos, 3 - Colo-Colo, 1 2
1 - 18 — Santos, 2 - Colombian All-Stars, 1 2
1 - 22 — Santos, 7 - Saprisa (Costa Rica), 3 1
1 - 25 — Santos, 3 - Herediano (Costa Rica), 0 1
1 - 29 — Santos, 4 - Guatemala All-Stars, 1 2
2 - 22 — Santos, 6 - América (Mexico), 2 2
3 - 5 — Santos, 3 - Fluminense, 1 2
3 - 11 — Santos, 7 - Flamengo, 1 3

144 **Appendixes**

4 - 1 — Santos, 4 - Botafogo (Rio), 2 2
4 - 5 — Santos, 3 - Atlético Mineiro, 1 2
4 - 10 — Santos, 6 - América (Rio), 1 1
6 - 1 — Santos, 8 - Basel (Basiléia), 2 2
6 - 3 — Santos, 6 - Wolfsburg (Germany), 3 2
6 - 7 — Santos, 6 - Racing (France), 1 2
6 - 9 — Santos, 6 - Olimpique Lyon, 2 2
6 - 11 — Santos, 1 - Tel Aviv–Israel All-Stars, 1 1
6 - 13 — Santos, 5 - Racing (France), 4 1
6 - 15 — Santos, 6 - Benfica, 3 2
6 - 18 — Santos, 3 - Juventus (Italy), 1 1
6 - 21 — Santos, 5 - Roma, 0 2
6 - 24 — Santos, 4 - Internazionale, 1 1
6 - 26 — Santos, 8 - Karlsrube (Germany), 6 3
6 - 28 — Santos, 3 - A.E.K. (Greece), 0 1
6 - 30 — Santos, 3 - Panathinaikos, 2 2
8 - 6 — Santos, 4 - Jabaquara, 0 1
8 - 9 — Santos, 3 - Guarani, 1 1
8 - 13 — Santos, 7 - Noroeste, 1 3
8 - 16 — Santos, 5 - Corintians, 1 1
8 - 19 — Santos, 6 - XV de Piracicaba, 1 3
8 - 30 — Santos, 8 - Olimpicos (Sta. Catarina), 0 5
9 - 3 — Santos, 6 - Sao Paulo, 3 4
9 - 6 — Santos, 10 - Juventus, 1 5
9 - 10 — Santos, 3 - Botafogo (Rib. Prêto), 0 1
9 - 13 — Santos, 5 - Esportiva de Guaratingueta, 1 4
9 - 17 — Santos, 6 - Portuguêsa Desportos, 1 4
9 - 28 — Santos, 4 - Racing (Argentina), 2 2
10 - 1 — Santos, 1 - Newell's (Argentina), 1 1
10 - 4 — Santos, 3 - Colo-Colo, 2 1
10 - 8 — Santos, 3 - Colo-Colo, 1 1
10 - 15 — Santos, 4 - Botafogo (Rib. Prêto), 1 1
10 - 13 — Santos, 5 - AA Portuguêsa, 2 2
10 - 28 — Santos, 3 - Portuguêsa Desportos, 1 2
11 - 1 — Santos, 3 - Juventus, 1 1
11 - 4 — Santos, 4 - Taubaté, 2 1
11 - 8 — Santos, 4 - Esportiva de Guaratingueta, 0 3
11 - 11 — Santos, 6 - América (Rio), 2 2
11 - 15 — Santos, 1 - Flamengo, 1 1

11 - 21 — Santos, 6 - América (Rio), 1 2
11 - 26 — Santos, 4 - Commercial, 1 1
11 - 29 — Santos, 2 - Palmeiras, 3 1
12 - 6 — Santos, 4 - Noroeste, 2 2
12 - 10 — Santos, 7 - XV de Piracicaba, 2 3
12 - 13 — Santos, 6 - Ferroviara, 2 2
12 - 16 — Santos, 4 - Sao Paulo, 1 1
12 - 27 — Santos, 5 - EC Bahia, 1 3

1962

1 - 14 — Santos, 6 - Dep. Universitario, 3 3
1 - 20 — Santos, 5 - Universitario, 2 1
1 - 24 — Santos, 5 - Esportivo Crystal, 1 1
1 - 28 — Santos, 3 - Deportivo Municipal, 2 1
1 - 31 — Santos, 3 - Nacional (Uruguay), 2 1
2 - 3 — Santos, 8 - Racing (Argentina), 3 1
2 - 14 — Santos, 3 - Seleçao Paulista Acesso, 1 1
2 - 28 — Santos, 9 - Cerro Porteno (Uruguay), 1 2
3 - 18 — Santos, 5 - Palmeiras, 3 2
4 - 21 — Brazil, 4 - Paraguay, 0 2
4 - 24 — Brazil, 6 - Paraguay, 0 1
5 - 9 — Brazil, 1 - Portugal, 0 1
5 - 12 — Brazil, 3 - Wales, 1 1
5 - 16 — Brazil, 3 - Wales, 1 2
5 - 30 — Brazil, 2 - Mexico, 0 1
8 - 5 — Santos, 2 - Prudentina, 1 1
8 - 12 — Santos, 4 - Palmeiras, 2 1
8 - 19 — Santos, 5 - Jabaquara, 1 3
8 - 26 — Santos, 1 - Guarani, 1 1
8 - 30 — Santos, 3 - Penarol (Uruguay), 0 2
9 - 2 — Santos, 3 - Sao Paulo, 3 2
9 - 5 — Santos, 5 - Botafogo (Rib. Prêto), 2 2
9 - 15 — Santos, 7 - Ferroviara, 2 4
9 - 19 — Santos, 3 - Benfica, 2 2
9 - 23 — Santos, 5 - Corintians, 2 1
9 - 26 — Santos, 4 - Noroeste, 0 2
9 - 30 — Santos, 3 - Comercial, 1 1

10 - 6 — Santos, 2 - Port. Desportos, 3 1
10 - 11 — Santos, 5 - Benfica, 2 3
10 - 17 — Santos, 5 - Racing (France), 2 2
10 - 20 — Santos, 3 - Hamburger, 3 2
10 - 22 — Santos, 4 - Sheffield Wedn, 2 1
10 - 27 — Santos, 3 - Taubaté, 0 1
10 - 31 — Santos, 5 - Guarani, 0 3
11 - 4 — Santos, 2 - Corintians, 1 1
11 - 7 — Santos, 3 - Juventus, 0 1
11 - 14 — Santos, 3 - Palmeiras, 0 1
11 - 21 — Santos, 4 - Port. Desportos, 1 2
11 - 28 — Santos, 6 - Comercial, 2 2
12 - 1 — Santos, 8 - Jabaquera, 2 4
12 - 5 — Santos, 5 - Sao Paulo, 2 1
12 - 10 — Santos, 2 - Russian All-Stars, 1 1
12 - 15 — Santos, 4 - Prudentina, 0 2

1963

1 - 9 — Santos, 3 - Seleçao de Sergipe, 2 2
1 - 23 — Santos, 2 - Colo-Colo, 1 2
1 - 30 — Santos, 8 - Deportivo de Lima, 3 3
2 - 2 — Santos, 2 - Alianza de Lima, 1 1
2 - 6 — Santos, 3 - Universidad de Lima, 4 2
2 - 10 — Santos, 5 - Clube Naval do Chile, 0 2
2 - 16 — Santos, 2 - Vasco da Gama, 2 2
2 - 20 — Santos, 6 - Português Desportos, 3 2
3 - 3 — Santos, 2 - Corintians, 0 2
3 - 7 — Santos, 6 - Sao Paulo, 2 3
3 - 16 — antos, 5 - Olaria, 1 3
3 - 19 — Santos, 4 - Botafogo (Rio), 3 2
3 - 23 — Santos, 2 - Fluminense, 4 1
3 - 27 — Santos, 3 - Flamengo, 0 1
4 - 2 — Santos, 5 - Botafogo (Rio), 0 2
4 - 16 — Brazil, 4 - Argentina, 1 3
4 - 27 — Brazil, 3 - France, 2 3
5 - 7 — Brazil, 2 - Germany, 1 1
5 - 29 — Santos, 3 - Hannover All-Stars, 2 1

6 - 2 — Santos, 2 - F. C. Schalke, 1 1
6 - 2 — Santos, 5 - Eintracht, 2 4
6 - 8 — Santos, 3 - V F Stuttgart, 1 1
6 - 15 — Santos, 4 - Roma, 3 2
6 - 26 — Santos, 3 - Juventus (Italy), 5 1
7 - 21 — Santos, 4 - Noroeste, 3 4
7 - 28 — Santos, 5 - Jabaquara, 2 1
7 - 31 — Santos, 2 - Esportiva Guaratingueta, 2 1
8 - 4 — Santos, 2 - Guarani, 1 1
8 - 15 — Santos, 1 - Sao Paulo, 4 1
8 - 22 — Santos, 1 - Botafogo (Rio), 1 1
8 - 28 — Santos, 4 - Botafogo (Rio), 0 3
9 - 1 — Santos, 1 - Ferroviara, 4 1
9 - 11 — Santos, 2 - Boca Juniors, 1 1
9 - 18 — Santos, 2 - Prudentina, 2 1
9 - 22 — Santos, 3 - Corintians, 1 3
9 - 29 — Santos, 3 - Botafogo (Rib. Prêto), 1 1
10 - 2 — Santos, 4 - Noroeste, 2 1
10 - 5 — Santos, 4 - Prudentina, 0 3
10 - 16 — Santos, 2 - Milan, 4 2
10 - 24 — Santos, 2 - Port. Desportos, 3 1
10 - 27 — Santos, 3 - Comercial, 0 2
10 - 30 — Santos, 2 - Sao Bento, 3 1

1964

1 - 16 — Santos, 3 - Grêmio Portoalegrense, 1 1
1 - 19 — Santos, 4 - Grêmio Portoalegrense, 3 3
1 - 25 — Santos, 6 - Bahia, 0 2
1 - 28 — Santos, 2 - Bahia, 0 2
2 - 22 — Santos, 3 - Sport Boys (Peru), 2 2
3 - 18 — Santos, 3 - Corintians, 0 1
4 - 25 — Santos, 3 - Botafogo (Rio), 1 1
5 - 1 — Santos, 2 - Flamengo, 3 1
5 - 5 — Santos, 4 - Boca Juniors, 3 1
5 - 7 — Santos, 2 - Racing (Argentina), 1 1
5 - 10 — Santos, 2 - Colon, 1 1
7 - 5 — Santos, 1 - América (Rio Prêto), 2 1

5 - 30 — Brazil, 5 - England, 1 1
6 - 7 — Brazil, 4 - Portugal, 1 1
8 - 19 — Santos, 6 - Guarani, 1 1
8 - 23 — Santos, 2 - Palmeiras, 1 1
9 - 23 — Santos, 1 - Sao Bento, 1 1
9 - 27 — Santos, 3 - Port. Desportos, 4 2
9 - 30 — Santos, 1 - Corintians, 1 1
10 - 4 — Santos, 3 - América (Rio Prêto), 1 1
10 - 7 — Santos, 1 - Colo-Colo, 3 1
10 - 14 — Santos, 3 - Comercial, 2 1
10 - 18 — Santos, 4 - Atlético Mineiro, 1 1
10 - 25 — Santos, 5 - Atlético Mineiro, 1 2
10 - 28 — Santos, 8 - Prudentina, 1 4
11 - 1 — Santos, 6 - XV de Piracicaba, 3 3
11 - 4 — Santos, 3 - Palmeiras, 2 1
11 - 21 — Santos, 11 - Botafogo (Rib. Prêto), 0 8
11 - 28 — Santos, 3 - Noroeste, 0 1
12 - 2 — Santos, 5 - Juventus, 2 2
12 - 6 — Santos, 7 - Corintians, 4 4
12 - 9 — Santos, 6 - Sao Bento, 0 3
12 - 16 — Santos, 4 - Flamengo, 1 3

1965

1 - 13 — Santos, 2 - Universidad Catolica, 1 1
1 - 16 — Santos, 6 - Czech All-Stars, 4 3
1 - 22 — Santos, 2 - River Plate, 3 1
2 - 2 — Santos, 3 - Universidade Chile, 0 1
2 - 9 — Santos, 4 - River Plate, 2 2
2 - 13 — Santos, 5 - Universidade Chile, 1 3
2 - 21 — Santos, 3 - Deportivo Galicia, 1 3
2 - 23 — Santos, 4 - Independiente, 0 2
2 - 25 — Santos, 1 - Universidade Chile, 0 1
3 - 6 — Santos, 2 - Universitario (Peru), 1 1
3 - 25 — Santos, 5 - Penarol, 4 1
3 - 31 — Santos, 1 - Penarol, 2 1
4 - 15 — Santos, 4 - Corintians, 4 4
4 - 18 — Santos, 5 - Fluminense, 2 1

4 - 29 — Santos, 9 - Clube do Reno, 4 5
5 - 2 — Santos, 6 - E. C. Bahia, 1 1
5 - 8 — Santos, 6 - Dom Bosco, 2 2
8 - 11 — Santos, 4 - Campo Grande, 1 2
5 - 14 — Santos, 2 - Olimpia (Paraguay), 2 1
5 - 16 — Santos, 11 - Maringa, 1 2
6 - 2 — Brazil, 5 - Belgium, 0 3
6 - 6 — Brazil, 2 - Germany, 0 1
6 - 17 — Brazil, 3 - Ora, 0 1
6 - 30 — Brazil, 3 - Russia, 0 2
7 - 14 — Santos, 6 - Noroeste, 2 5
7 - 18 — Santos, 3 - Ferroviaria, 1 3
7 - 21 — Santos, 5 - Commercial, 3 3
7 - 26 — Santos, 6 - G. R. Brasil (Maceio), 0 4
7 - 28 — Santos, 3 - Santo Antônio (Vitoria), 1 1
8 - 4 — Santos, 2 - A. A. Portuguêsa, 0 1
8 - 8 — Santos, 4 - Bocas Juniors, 1 2
8 - 12 — Santos, 2 - River Plate, 1 1
8 - 15 — Santos, 3 - Prudentina, 1 3
8 - 22 — Santos, 4 - Portuguêsa de Desportos, 0 3
8 - 29 — Santos, 4 - Corintians, 3 2
9 - 4 — Santos, 7 - Botafogo, 1 3
9 - 8 — Santos, 3 - Juventus, 1 2
9 - 11 — Santos, 7 - Guarani, 0 4
10 - 3 — Santos, 3 - Noroeste, 0 1
10 - 7 — Santos, 4 - Sao Bento, 2 1
10 - 10 — Santos, 2 - Commercial, 0 1
10 - 13 — Santos, 3 - A. A. Portuguêsa, 0 1
10 - 24 — Santos, 4 - América, 0 3
10 - 31 — Santos, 5 - Prudentina, 2 5
11 - 10 — Santos, 1 - Palmeiras (Brazilian Cup), 1 1
11 - 14 — Santos, 4 - Corintians, 1 1
11 - 21 — Brazil, 2 - Russia, 2 1
11 - 25 — Santos, 5 - Botafogo (RP), 0 4
11 - 27 — Santos, 4 - Juventus, 0 3
11 - 4 — Santos, 1 - Guarani, 0 1
12 - 8 — Santos, 1 - Vasco (Brazilian Cup), 0 1

1966

1 - 9 — Santos, 7 - Stad Club (Abidjan), 0 2
1 - 14 — Santos, 2 - Comb. Tucuman, 0 1
1 - 16 — Santos, 1 - Alianza (El Salvador), 2 1
1 - 19 — Santos, 1 - Botafogo (in Caracas), 2 1
1 - 26 — Santos, 2 - Universitario (Lima), 2 1
1 - 29 — Santos, 4 - Alianza (Lima), 1 1
2 - 9 — Santos, 6 - Universidad (Chile), 1 3
2 - 17 — Santos, 2 - Colo-Colo (Chile), 2 1
3 - 29 — Santos, 3 - Cruzeiro, 4 1
3 - 31 — Santos, 1 - Atlético Mineiro, 0 1
6 - 4 — Brazil, 4 - Peru, 0 1
6 - 12 — Brazil, 2 - Czechoslovakia, 1 1
6 - 15 — Brazil, 2 - Czechoslovakia, 2 1
6 - 21 — Brazil, 5 - Atlético de Madrid, 3 3
7 - 4 — Brazil, 4 - AIK, 2 2
7 - 6 — Brazil, 3 - Malmœ, 1 2
7 - 12 — Brazil, 2 - Bulgaria, 0 1
8 - 21 — Santos, 4 - Benfica, 0 1
8 - 31 — Santos, 2 - Atlante, 2 1
9 - 4 — Santos, 4 - Internazionale, 1 1
9 - 11 — Santos, 3 - Prudentina, 1 2
10 - 16 — Santos, 2 - Sao Bento, 2 1
10 - 23 — Santos, 4 - Noroeste, 1 2
10 - 26 — Santos, 3 - A. A. Portuguêsa, 0 1
10 - 30 — Santos, 1 - Sao Paulo, 2 1
11 - 5 — Santos, 3 - Juventus, 0 1
11 - 9 — Santos, 2 - Nautico (Brazilian Cup), 0 1
11 - 13 — Santos, 3 - Bragantino, 2 3
12 - 4 — Santos, 3 - Botafogo, 1 1
12 - 7 — Santos, 2 - Cruzeiro, 3 1

1967

1 - 19 — Santos, 4 - River Plate, 0 1
1 - 29 — Santos, 2 - River Plate, 4 2
2 - 1 — Santos, 2 - River Plate, 1 1

2 - 11 — Santos, 2 - Vasas, 2 1
2 - 21 — Santos, 6 - U. Calotica, 2 4
2 - 25 — Santos, 4 - Alianza (Lima), 1 1
3 - 15 — Santos, 5 - Internacional, 1 1
3 - 12 — Santos, 4 - Grêmio, 1 1
3 - 26 — Santos, 1 - Vasco, 2 1
4 - 1 — Santos, 1 - Sao Paulo, 1 1
4 - 15 — Santos, 2 - Portuguêsa de Desportos, 2 2
4 - 23 — Santos, 3 - Bangu, 0 1
5 - 4 — Santos, 3 - Feroviaria, 0 1
5 - 7 — Santos, 3 - Selec. Ilheus, 1 1
5 - 10 — Santos, 5 - Santa Cruz, 0 1
5 - 13 — Santos, 1 - Corintians, 1 1
5 - 23 — Santos, 3 - Portuguêsa de Desportos, 2 2
5 - 25 — Santos, 5 - Comb. Brasilia, 1 1
5 - 28 — Santos, 4 - Selec. Senegal, 1 3
5 - 31 — Santos, 4 - Selec. Ojabao, 0 2
6 - 2 — Santos, 2 - Selec. Congo, 1 1
6 - 4 — Santos, 2 - Selec. Costa do Marfim, 1 1
6 - 7 — Santos, 3 - Selec. Brazzaville, 2 3
6 - 13 — Santos, 5 - TVS-Munchen, 4 2
6 - 16 — Santos, 2 - Mantova, 1 1
6 - 24 — Santos, 5 - Lecce, 1 3
6 - 29 — Santos, 3 - Roma, 1 1
7 - 9 — Santos, 4 - Sao Bento, 3 1
7 - 15 — Santos, 4 - Juventus, 0 1
8 - 6 — Santos, 1 - Palmeiras, 1 1
8 - 19 — Santos, 4 - Comercial, 1 1
10 - 8 — Santos, 3 - América, 2 1
10 - 17 — Santos, 2 - Sao Paulo, 2 1
10 - 22 — Santos, 4 - Prudentina, 1 2
10 - 29 — Santos, 4 - Palmeiras, 1 1
11 - 7 — Santos, 5 - Combinado Cearense, 0 1
11 - 11 — Santos, 1 - Comercial, 1 1
12 - 3 — Santos, 1 - Guarani, 1 1
12 - 10 — Santos, 2 - Corintians, 1 1
12 - 17 — Santos, 3 - A. A. Portuguêsa, 1 1

1968

1 - 23 — Santos, 4 - Vasas (Hungary), 0 1

3 - 3 — Santos, 4 - Ferroviaria, 1 2

3 - 9 — Santos, 5 - Botafogo, 1 1

3 - 16 — Santos, 3 - Portuguêsa de Desportos, 0 1

3 - 19 — Santos, 3 - E. C. Goias, 3 1

3 - 23 — Santos, 4 - Juventus, 0 2

3 - 27 — Santos, 5 - Sao Paulo, 2 2

3 - 31 — Santos, 4 - América, 3 2

4 - 7 — Santos, 8 - Comercial, 2 2

4 - 21 — Santos, 2 - Corintians, 0 1

4 - 24 — Santos, 3 - Juventus, 2 2

5 - 19 — Santos, 3 - Pameiras, 1 1

5 - 29 — Santos, 5 - Comercial, 0 1

6 - 12 — Santos, 2 - Alessandria, 1 1

6 - 15 — Santos 4 - Zurich, 5 1

6 - 17 — Santos, 3 - Saar All-Stars, 0 1

6 - 21 — Santos, 4 - Naples, 2 1

6 - 26 — Santos, 6 - Naples, 2 2

6 - 28 — Santos, 5 - Naples, 2 2

6 - 30 — Santos, 3 - Saint Louis, 2 1

7 - 4 — Santos, 4 - Kansas City Spurs, 1 1

7 - 6 — Santos, 4 - Necaxa, 3 1

7 - 8 — Santos, 7 - Boston Beacons, 1 1

7 - 21 — Santos, 4 - Sel. Olimpica Colômbia, 2 1

7 - 25 — Brazil, 4 - Paraguay, 0 2

8 - 6 — Santos, 3 - Paissandu, 1 1

8 - 9 — Santos, 3 - Nacional-Fast, 0 1

8 - 11 — Santos, 2 - Nacional (Manaus), 1 1

8 - 20 — Santos, 2 - Nacional (Uruguay), 2 1

8 - 28 — Santos, 6 - Cleveland, 2 3

8 - 30 — Santos, 3 - Oakland Clippers, 1 2

9 - 21 — Santos, 2 - Fluminense, 1 1

10 - 6 — Santos, 2 - Corintians, 1 1

10 - 10 — Santos, 9 - E. C. Bahia, 2 3

10 - 13 — Santos, 2 - Cruzeiro, 0 1

10 - 23 — Santos, 3 - Internacional (PA), 1 1

10 - 27 — Santos, 3 - Nautico, 0 1
11 - 13 — Brazil, 2 - Mexico, 1 1
11 - 19 — Santos, 2 - Racing (Argentina), 0 1
11 - 24 — Santos, 2 - Atlético Mineiro, 2 1
11 - 27 — Santos, 2 - Grêmio Porto-Alegrense, 1 1
12 - 4 — Santos, 2 - Internacional (PA), 1 1
12 - 10 — Santos, 2 - Vasco, 1 1
12 - 17 — Brazil, 3 - Yugoslavia, 3 1

1969

1 - 17 — Santos, 3 - Sel. Point Noire, 0 1
1 - 19 — Santos, 3 - Sel. do Congo, 2 2
1 - 23 — Santos, 2 - Sel. Congo-Kinshasa, 3 2
1 - 26 — Santos, 2 - Aguias Verdes Lagos, 2 2
2 - 6 — Santos, 2 - Hearts of Oak Accra, 2 1
2 - 14 — Santos, 6 - XV de Piracicaba, 2 2
2 - 22 — Santos, 4 - Portuguêsa de Desportos, 1 1
2 - 26 — Santos, 3 - Ferroviara, 0 2
3 - 9 — Santos, 3 - Sao Paulo, 0 1
3 - 12 — Santos, 4 - Sao Bento, 2 2
3 - 15 — Santos, 2 - Juventus, 1 1
3 - 23 — Santos, 2 - Palmeiras, 3 2
3 - 26 — Santos, 4 - Botafogo, 1 1
3 - 29 — Santos, 3 - A.A. Portuguêsa, 1 3
4 - 9 — Brazil, 3 - Peru, 2 1
4 - 27 — Santos, 1 - América, 1 1
4 - 30 — Santos, 1 - A.A. Portuguêsa, 2 1
5 - 11 — Santos, 1 - Ferroviara, 2 1
5 - 28 — Santos, 3 - Paulista, 2 1
5 - 31 — Santos, 5 - Botafogo, 1 4
6 - 8 — Santos, 3 - Corintians, 1 2
6 - 18 — Santos, 3 - Palmeiras, 0 1
7 - 6 — Brazil, 4 - Bahia, 0 1
7 - 13 — Brazil, 6 - Pernambuco, 1 1
8 - 10 — Brazil, 5 - Colombia, 0 2
8 - 21 — Brazil, 6 - Colombia, 2 1
8 - 24 — Brazil, 6 - Venezuela, 0 2

8 - 30 — Brazil, 1 - Paraguay, 0 1
9 - 3 — Brazil, 1 - Atlético Mineiro, 2 1
9 - 10 — Santos, 3 - Estrêla Vermelha, 3 1
9 - 15 — Santos, 4 - Radnicki, 4 1
9 - 19 — Santos, 1 - Zeleznicar, 1 1
9 - 22 — Santos, 3 - Stoke City, 2 2
9 - 24 — Santos, 7 - Comb. Sampdoria-Gênova, 1 2
9 - 28 — Santos, 1 - Grêmio Portoalegrense 2 1
10 - 12 — Santos, 1 - Palmeiras, 2 1
10 - 15 — Santos, 6 - Portuguêsa de Desportos, 2 4
10 - 22 — Santos, 3 - Coritiba, 1 2
11 - 1 — Santos, 4 - Flamengo, 1 1
11 - 13 — Santos, 4 - Santa Cruz, 0 2
11 - 14 — Santos, 3 - Botafogo (Paraiba), 0 1
11 - 19 — Santos, 2 - Vasco, 1 1

The Top Scorers of the Brazilian Team

The figures concern the matches played by the Brazilian national team since 1934. In parentheses, the period during which they wore the colors of the national team.

1. Pelé : 90 goals
2. Tostao : 34
3. Ademir : 32 (40/50)
4. Jaïrzinho : 31
5. Zizinho : 26 (40/50)
6. Leonidas : 23 (30/40)
7. Pepe : 23 (50/60)
8. Jair R. P. : 21 (40/50)
9. Didi : 20 (50–60)
10. Rivelino : 20
11. Baltazar : 17 (40/50)
12. Quarentinha : 17 (50/60)
13. Vava : 15 (50/60)
14. Heleno : 15 (40)

15. Garrincha : 15
16. Gerson : 15
17. Julinho : 13 (50/60)
18. Tesourinha : 10 (40)
19. Amarildo : 9
20. Chinezinho : 9
21. Pinga : 9 (50)
22. Evaristo : 8 (50)
23. Waldemar de Brito : 7 (30) (the one who discovered Pelé)
24. Carlos Alberto : 7
25. Coutinho : 7
26. Chico : 7
27. Altafini : 7

The Brazilian Internationals

Those who have worn the colors of Brazil most frequently since 1934, that is, since the early years of Brazil's participation in the World Cup.

1. Djal. Santos	110	36. Danieol	25	71. Mengalvio	15
2. Pelé	108	37. Clodoaldo	25	72. Manga	15
3. Gilmar	99	38. Everaldo	25	73. Coutinho	15
4. Nilt. Santos	81	39. Leonidas	24	74. Paul. Borges	15
5. Didi	72	40. Tesourinha	23	75. J. Martins	15
6. Gerson	72	41. Vava	22	76. Dorval	14
7. Jaïrzinho	66	42. Altaïr	22	77. Maurinho	14
8. Garrincha	58	43. Rober. Dias	22	78. Jurandir (SP)	14
9. Bellini	56	44. Dino Sani	21	79. Carv. Leite	14
10. Tostao	54	45. Patesko	21	80. Natal	14
11. Carl. Alberto	53	46. Norival	20	81. Jaime	14
12. Zizinho	53	47. Z. Procopio	20	82. Djal. Dias	13
13. Zito	51	48. Chinezinho	20	83. Evaristo	13
14. Brito	48	49. Barbosa	19	84. Romeu	13
15. Rildo	45	50. Chico	19	85. Edson (America)	13
16. Rivelino	45	51. Rodrigues	19	86. Martin	12
17. Pepe	41	52. Canhoteiro	19	87. Claudio (Corint.)	12
18. Félix	39	53. Lima	19	88. Dirc. Lopes	12
19. Jaïr da R.P.	38	54. Alfonsinho	19	89. Friaça	12
20. Ad. Menzes	38	55. Heleno	18	90. Dudu	12
21. Zagalo	37	56. Augusto	18	91. Oreco	11
22. Piazza	36	57. Brandaozinho	18	92. Sady	11
23. Zozimo	35	58. Luisinho	18	93. P. Henrique	11
24. Edu (Sant.)	34	59. Pinga	18	94. Luizinho T.	11
25. Orlando	32	60. Quarentinha	18	95. Denilson	11
26. Paulo Cesar	32	61. Pinheiro	17	96. Canalli	10
27. Julinho	30	62. R. Belangero	17	97. Argemiro	10
28. Mauro	29	63. Zequinha (Pal.)	17	98. Bigode	10
29. Joel Camargo	29	64. Ely	17	99. Jau	10
30. Castilho	28	65. Formiga	16	100. Eduardo, Calvet,
31. Rui	28	66. Tim	16	Roberto (Botaf.),
32. Domin. da Guia	27	67. Flavio	16	Eduardo (Penta Esq.),
33. Palthazar	27	68. Noronha	16	Parana and Altafini each
34. Bauer	27	69. M. Antonio	16	also 10 selections.
35. Amarildo	26	70. Brandao	16		

What They Think of Pelé

M. LEPRINCE-RINGUET

Professor at the Collège de France

I believe that the success and the popularity of Pelé constitute a specific Brazilian phenomenon, for soccer is of immense importance there to the young and especially to the poor, because it offers them social advancement, helps them get out of their condition. In France the young can direct their potential into various fields.

As for his universal popularity, aside from his obviously exceptional qualities as a soccer player, it seems to me he possesses a kind of presence that makes people look at him and like him.

LEO WEINSTEIN
Professor of literature, Stanford University, California
I have had the good fortune to follow Pelé since his first World Cup match in 1958. What makes him unique is his electrifying effect on the crowd every time he touches the ball. You know something unusual is going to happen and it always does, even when his attempt does not succeed.

Some of his exploits have been immortalized by the camera. A sequence often featured on U.S. television shows him pushing the ball successively between the legs of two onrushing defenders, then faking out a third one with a sudden stop and change of direction before shooting at goal. But no camera can capture the excitement of watching the number one soccer player (who has never had to proclaim himself the best) in live action on the field.

ANDRÉ HELARD
Agrégé professor of letters
. . . Because with him soccer becomes an art. For fifteen years Pelé has given all those who believe in soccer reasons for hope. To see Pelé play is to rediscover the happiness of the game, for beyond his immense individual talent he has the genius of revealing the true nature of soccer and its *raison d'être*—to reaffirm that the soccer player, like any other human being, realizes himself only by placing his genius at the service of all in order to accomplish the common enterprise.

DR. LIONEL LONGUEVILLE
Specialist in sports medicine
I believe that the shot from 65 yards which Pelé attempted in the 1970 World Cup gives an idea of what kind of a player he is. An immediate reading of the game, a sudden inspiration, an instantaneous

reflex, uncommon technical means. Unfortunately, I have seen Pelé only on television. But that action enables me to say that he is a soccer player with exceptional intelligence. There are no great champions without intelligence.

MARC BOGTANOVITCH
Architect, city planner
For me Pelé is an unusual phenomenon, because he produces a collective delirium in millions of people.

ARAUJO NETTO
Brazilian writer
Pelé is a maniac for perfection. One who is forever dissatisfied, for whom victories and the first place are not enough if they are not surrounded with exceptional circumstances and merits. . . . The master of nerves of steel, and with an almost homicidal aggressiveness at the crucial and decisive moment of a competition, he has remained human to the point of having stayed as he was in 1958: a good son, a good brother, a pleasant companion, a loyal friend. . . . In the brief history of the King of States, the extraordinary becomes a commonplace. Nothing that happens to Pelé can surprise us. Even when the papers announce that the all-powerful General Charles de Gaulle has made him a Knight of the Order of Merit, we are no longer astonished. We say at most that France has offered the world another confirmation of its good taste and its intelligence.

(*Brasil Futebol Rei*, 1965).

JEAN-PIERRE LEMAUX
Engineer
Although medical instruments are capable of analyzing and comparing Pelé's physical gifts with those of other athletic champions, the aptitudes that distinguish him and delight the crowds are neither measurable nor quantifiable, for they border on art.

JEAN-CLAUDE BRIALY
Actor
Pelé . . . *Ah oui*, what an artist! In our profession I compare him to Gérard Philipe. He is endowed with such grace. I have had the

great pleasure of meeting him in Rio and of seeing him play with his Santos team. What an orchestra leader!

JACQUES CHARRIER
Actor

I have had the pleasure of seeing Pelé in action in Rio and in Paris. I had some idea of soccer, having kicked a ball when I was a kid and later in the "Scotchmen," a team managed by my friend Gilles Durieux. Seeing Pelé play, I had the impression that he was playing a sport other than soccer. He attracts the ball—it sticks to him as if by magic. He is an acrobat, a magician. There is as much difference between him and the other players (except perhaps Johan Cruyff) as between Lêo Ferré and Dalida in the field of song.

PIERRE MASSIMI
Actor

Pelé is a great artist. I don't know him as a person, but when one plays the way he does, that is to say, when one possesses such intelligence in the game, one can only be a nice guy. In a different style Cruyff reminds me of him. But he is a product of European soccer. Pelé improvises like the jazz artists.

FRANÇOIS CHAUMETTE
Sociétaire of the Comédie Française

At the time when soccer was an offensive and spectacular game, I used to go regularly to the Parc des Princes and I have had a chance to admire Pelé during the Paris Tournaments. The Santos players used to give the impression that they were having a good time on the field and Pelé led the ballet with a fantastic precision and a spirit of unselfishness. Today defensive tactics have killed the offensive spirit of the game and the soccer of Pelé, Gudmundsson, Amalfi, Piantoni has turned into a boring spectacle. One has the impression of being in a lecture hall. I no longer find the time to watch it, not even on television.

CLAUDE BRASSEUR
Actor

I have often seen Pelé play and what has always struck me in him, aside from the fact that he belongs to Brazilian soccer, the most beautiful in the world, is his extraordinary appetite for goals. I believe he said one day that he compared the scoring of a goal to the sexual act. A player as gifted as he can play any position brilliantly. But I wonder whether he would have played soccer in any role other than that of forward.

CLAUDE NOUGARO
Singer

Like everybody, I know Pelé. Or rather, I only know his fabulous aspect. He is more than a soccer player, he is an artist, for what he does on the field borders on art.

CLAUDE GUILHOT
Jazz vibraphone player

I think that what strikes one most in him is his universality. By himself he is Di Stefano, Puskas, Matthews, Kopa, Fontaine. . . . Like a great actor it seems he can play every role. . . . Will he use his ability to jump high, his speed (like a huge deer), his phenomenal technique, or will he be content with the little, decisive pass that his reading of the game inspires him to make? Whatever he does, in my view he embodies both soccer and its genius.

JACQUES DI DONATO
Clarinet soloist, first prize of the Paris Conservatory

A soccer player of genius endowed with exceptional vision and intelligence, Pelé is the finest example of the offensive player. But is it possible to defend one's art when one is constantly the object of aggressions?

PIERRE CHARLES BAYLE
Artist

An extraordinary technique at the service of originality in the conception of their work—these are the qualities that enable certain artists to attain the status of universal genius. Pelé—one of the rare "figures" to possess these two qualities fully in his sport or art—attains genius in his great moments.

M. GREARD

Air France long-distance pilot

Pelé, ten years ago. Maracana Rio. A match Botafogo-Santos. The crowd, colors, a passionate atmosphere. This young genius of a "jogador" is just a delight. A dream goal. Pelé controls a center from the left with his chest and shoots with his right foot before the ball touches the ground. Goal. Firecrackers bursting forth even from the ranks of the Botafogo supporters. What soccer and what a life. Pelé, a dream player! *Que maravilhosa!*

DANIEL HECHTER

Dress designer

Pelé. First of all he's a personality, in life, and it comes out on the field. As an athlete he is the sort that I call a super-champion. He has something more than the others. Even Di Stefano did not have that faculty of "going into a higher gear," of executing what the others couldn't manage to perceive. Soccer players like Pelé, there's one every generation, and even at that . . .

JOAO QUARTIM

Brazilian student

Like all Brazilians, I love soccer and I admire the great soccer player Pelé. On the political level, it is a fact that the régime has made abundant use of his success, his prestige, of the image of success provided by the rise of this very poor young Black, who comes from the interior of the country. An image he has done nothing to tone down, even though he shows more sensitivity than others about his origins. But one can't consider this problem in extreme terms. Because of their very modest origins, the Brazilian soccer players are not ideologically equipped to take a position like those who come from a culturally more developed environment. And if one agrees that Pelé's passive behavior over the policies of the current Brazilian governments constitutes objectively a political attitude, one must also agree that his refusal to participate in the 1974 World Cup, as requested by these governments, also constitutes, objectively, a political attitude.

JEAN LEVRON

Official at the Treasury Department

Pelé means incomparable personal gifts used for the good of the team and never for his own good. Pelé means the stroke of genuis that is evident to everybody . . . afterwards. He is the complete soccer player, who links this sport with intelligence. And with art.

ANDRÉ ANFRY
Typographer
I discovered Pelé in 1958 on television and I was dazzled—I believe that is the word for the game he played against France. I saw him again in Paris when he played there with Santos and, of course, during the 1970 World Cup. I am a former player and I very much appreciated players like Jonquet and Kopa. But Pelé, now that's something else. . . . Everybody's soccer favorite.

MAURICE PUJOL
Carpenter
I know that Pelé has scored more than 1,000 goals and that is tremendous. But what I like most in him is the accuracy of his passes and his team spirit. The wall passes with Coutinho in the Paris Tournaments, that's something I believe I'll never forget. . . .

GABRIELLE WATRIN
Secretary
Pelé is the man who turns a match into a festive occasion on the field and in the stands. To a casual spectator it seems that everything is easy for him, that he can get out of the most difficult situations, and that he is having an awfully good time.

JEAN-CLAUDE MANSARD
Schoolboy, twelve years old
When I was younger, in the games we played in courtyards, we would take the names of great players. I never managed to get Pelé's, because it was always taken. . . .

BOBBY MOORE
Former captain of England's national team
I knew that the day they let Pelé play a World Cup his way, he would win it as easily as breathing.

TOSTAO

Pelé's teammate on the 1970 Brazilian team

All my life I shall be grateful to Joao Saldanha for having given me the chance to play next to Pelé. That was my dream and when it came true, it was even more beautiful. Nothing is easier than to play on his team, because he frees you in every way by attracting the opponents' attention, by inspiring in you the move that has to be made. Among soccer's greats there is Pelé and then the others. He cannot be compared with anybody.

CARLOS ALBERTO

Pelé's teammate and captain of the 1970 Brazilian team

When he retires from soccer, nothing will be as it was before. . . .

RAYMOND KOPA

France's best-known player, retired

I do not know Pelé personally. I can only judge him by what I have seen. He is truly the greatest. I have seen him do things that no one but he could execute. His technical feats are those of an acrobat and it's not enough to explain them by saying that he is skillful, catlike, astute, keen. That he is an instinctive player with exceptional physical qualities, diabolical self-control, dexterity, and precision, everybody knows. Pelé is no doubt the only player who defies analysis, whom reason does not explain. For me, there is a mystery about Pelé in this respect; he is at the same time animal-like and intelligent, instinctive and also deliberate. He possesses genius, but his genius is not produced by instinct. There is something else. What is it? I've no idea.

(*Mon Football*—Calmann-Levy Publishers)

FERENC PUSKAS

Captain of Hungarian team, later Real Madrid, retired

When I finished my career as a player, one of my greatest regrets was that I did not succeed in performing three or four technical exploits I saw him do. I failed because he is a soccer player who cannot be compared with any other one.

JUST FONTAINE

Record World Cup scorer, now coach

If good fairies of soccer exist, they all got together around Pelé's cradle and showered him with gifts. This feline, this black panther contains all the qualities soccer demands. His speed, his jumping ability, his head play, his shooting, and his reading of the game are dazzling. He is unadulterated dash, the god of Soccer who came down from Mount Olympus to preach on earth, the natural player, naturally endowed with the rarest of gifts. . . . Can you charge him even once, one single and solitary time, with an error in position play? Has he sinned by being too individualistic, has he spoiled a scoring chance? Has he permitted himself a crime of lèse-soccer? If someone has knowledge of some such miracle, let him make it known without delay. We would all sleep better and feel more at ease.

(*La reprise de volée*—Solar Publishers)

RACHID MEKHLOUFI
Former professional in France, now Algerian national coach

What we call class in soccer is intelligence which, in my opinion, cannot be separated from simplicity. To me Pelé is the very symbol of class, because he is intelligent on the field but also in everything he does in life. I had the opportunity to talk with him after a game between Algeria and Brazil played at Oran. When I congratulated him and asked him: "How do you do it, play that way?" he replied in the most natural manner in the world: "What about you? You play as well as I."

NORBERT ESCHMANN
Former Swiss international, now journalist

1959. Santos is finishing a triumphal tour at Geneva. Being a professional at the Olympique de Marseilles at the time, I am asked to help out the Servette team. The coach warns me: "You play in midfield on the right and the name of the number 10 opposite you is Pelé." Santos leads 1–0 and seems satisfied to hold that lead. Twenty minutes before the end, on a pass from Fatton, I beat Gilmar. Are we happy? And how! After all, those Brazilians are not so terrific. And like any other player, Pelé can be tired. But Pelé is not satisfied. He argues with his teammates and, as they kick off, he seems to give some orders. Now the machine starts to function. . . . From everywhere "they" come at us. In Pelé's zone I haul in air. I don't remember exactly what he did, but it soon became clear to me that the ball was out of reach for me.

On a center I jump into the air with him. As high as I possibily could. Pelé sort of stopped in mid-air. Like a god. Then he faked a head shot. Our goalie René Schneider, who was excellent in anticipation, dived into the corner. Whereupon Pelé headed the ball into the opposite corner. Into the one where Schneider was not. I have never seen such a goal nor such a scene. Santos waved at the delighted crowd. Pelé smiled. So did we. 4–1; we had understood.

JULIO MAZZEI
Former Santos trainer, now Pelé's personal trainer
I am sure that if Pelé had specialized in track and field, he would be one of the ten best decathlon competitors in the world; for he has all the characteristics of the complete athlete: speed, a quick start, resistance, power.

JEAN-PIERRE DOGLIANI
Player on team of Paris-Saint Germain
I was a junior player in Marseilles the first time I saw him play in 1960, and I was playing in the preliminary game of the Reims-Santos match. When I saw him warm up near the dressing rooms, he seemed to me like a kid. He was laughing while accomplishing little technical exploits and enjoying the horseplay. His youth and his apparent fragility had struck me forcibly. But on the field I saw that this "kid" took on a different dimension. And all the superlatives one can think of fail to express what he accomplishes. He made me understand then that soccer can become an extraordinary means of expression and that physical appearance is of little importance where soccer is concerned.

There is only one Pelé, a creative genius, but each soccer player carries within him the possibility of creation and change. If I could see him again one day, I shall thank him, for he made me discover soccer and the player who is an artist, a creator.

OSWALDO ZUBELDIA
Argentine coach
Watch when a team scores a goal. The player who made the decisive pass does not embrace anybody. He returns all alone to the center of the field as if he did not want to attach any importance to his contribution in the scoring of the goal, whereas in reality he stays apart

so that the spectators will notice him and say: "He is the one who made the decisive pass." . . . In the 1970 Mundial Pelé offered numerous goals to his partners. But when everybody embraced after the goals, he took part in it with the others. There is all the difference. . . .

JO MASO
Rugby international

I met Pelé in Australia where the French rugby team and Santos were both on tour; I watched two of his games, I talked with him. He was saturated with soccer after a long series of games. But he made an extraordinary impression on me. He was there to make the others play. Every play turned around him, but he never tried to shine. Only once did he dribble to eliminate three opponents simultaneously. I followed his World Cup matches on television. He is a player who can do everything. Some great players have physical or technical limitations. One has the impression that for him nothing is impossible.

DANTE PANZERI
Argentine TV sportscaster

One does not learn soccer either from books or from a technical director's instructions. Soccer is learned by playing, in the joy of the game. That is why Brazil has the best soccer in the world and produces the finest geniuses in the game.

OSWALDO ARDIZZONE
Journalist, Buenos Aires *El Grafico*

Pelé gave the ultimate message of his genius by placing the ball on Carlos Alberto's right foot—and so he wrote the 1970 Mundial's glorious epilogue. What an example! What an example for those who brag aloud on the dangerous Olympus of renown.

O Estado de Sao Paulo
Sao Paulo daily

The young and the children recognize themselves in Pelé's smile. It is purity, vivaciousness, the gracefulness of life itself that comes and goes. It is also simplicity. The spontaneous smile of a child that covers a great amount of fellow feeling.

The Sunday Times
London
   "How do you write Pelé?"
   "G.O.D."

Daily Telegraph
London
   He has become a legend, who surpasses himself and creates moments of magic.

ROBERT NATAF
Journalist (*France-Soir*)
   Pelé is the magic of the . . . natural. This is in no way a paradox. Thanks to him, soccer has rediscovered its original virtues, thought to have been buried forever beneath the rubbish of so-called modernism or realism. Thanks to Pelé, the natural gesture has been recognized and rehabilitated. There is the magic; the indelible image King Pelé will leave behind.

LOUIS LUCCHESI
Reporter-photographer
   I am not a soccer specialist, but I have had the opportunity to do some articles on Pelé and I can say, strictly on the professional level, that there are few great international stars who show as much kindness and comprehension. I especially recall a chance encounter with him at Guadeloupe, where Santos was resting from the fatigue of a long tour. Although under those circumstances he obviously was in need of relaxation and calmness, he did all he could to facilitate the execution of my task.

TEX MAULE
Journalist, *Sports Illustrated*
   Unlike many virtuosi, Pelé is obviously no prima donna. In the modern sports era of the overpaid egoist, he is unfailingly gracious, charming and patient. . . .
   The Cosmos can take a tax loss on any remaining deficit at the end of the year. . . . But Pelé is worth all they paid for him just as a goodwill ambassador for soccer. And as a breath of fresh air in professional sports.